MINISTERIAL
ETHICS AND
ETIQUETTE

SECOND REVISED EDITION

MINISTERIAL
ETHICS AND
ETIQUETTE

NOLAN B.
HARMON

ABINGDON PRESS
Nashville

MINISTERIAL ETHICS AND ETIQUETTE

Library of Congress Cataloging-in-Publication Data

Harmon, Nolan B. (Nolan Bailey), 1892-
  Ministerial ethics and etiquette.
  1. Pastoral theology. 2. Clergy—Etiquette.
  I. Title.
  BV4012.H3   1987   174'.1   87-12604

ISBN 0-687-27034-0 (alk. paper)

All scripture quotations, unless otherwise noted, are from the King James
Version of the Bible.

Those noted RSV are from the Revised Standard Version of the Bible
copyrighted 1946, 1951, © 1971, 1973 by the Division of Christian
Education of the National Council of the Churches of Christ in the
U.S.A., and are used by permission.

MANUFACTURED BY THE PARTHENON PRESS AT
NASHVILLE, TENNESSEE, UNITED STATES OF AMERICA

To the Memory of
MY MOTHER
JULIET HOWE HARMON

Who Taught Me
Ways of Gentleness
As Well As
Christian Living

CONTENTS

MINISTERIAL
ETHICS AND
ETIQUETTE

INTRODUCTION

It has long been our conviction that a minister, if a man, must always be a gentleman; if a woman, a lady. This should almost go without saying. Thus we assume that a true Christian, man or woman, will instinctively know how to behave almost everywhere. This does not mean that the moment a minister is consecrated to God he or she will automatically know "which fork to use first" or understand all the vagaries of social protocol. The fashion of this world changes and so do the pretty—and petty—customs that prevail among ladies and gentlemen. But beneath the whole range of matters discussed in the "Blue Book"— knives and forks, soup and fish, the cutting of cabbages and the treatment of kings—there are a few deep principles. These principles, the postulates upon which gentle people act, are not far from a Christian ethic. A gentleman may not be a Christian, but a Christian must always be a gentleman. If urbane people of the world can achieve a high plane of courtesy and honor, surely the men and women of God can do no less. Old, naive, unsophisticated ministers, ignorant of all the customs of polite society but saturated with the grace of God through years of service, sometimes show in face and bearing a graceful tenderness and an air of Christian courtliness that the halls of Versailles might well have envied. *Unselfishness,* or a pretense to it, underlies the whole code of proper conduct in the "Blue Book," but with the Christian it cannot be pretense. Taking thought for others is the essence of ministerial ethics and etiquette.

Until comparatively recent years, no serious attempt was made to draw up anything like a code of ministerial ethics. In the very nature of things, nothing like a binding code of ethical conduct can be drawn, for it would be impossible to get general agreement among ministers on many points having to do with manners and morals. Many churches and sects today cannot agree on some of the greater moral issues. How then can they be expected to agree on minor matters having to do with moot points of ethical conduct or, in some instances, mere etiquette? Furthermore, even if there were agreement on these matters, there is not and cannot be any interdenominational court or tribunal to force on any minister a system governing morals or conduct. They are a law unto themselves. If their fathers went to war to prevent some church or king from telling them how they should kneel or sit or stand at Communion, they are not going to let anyone today tell them how to make a pastoral call or what church publicity they may properly use. The whole system of Protestantism is wound up with the individual's rights in this matter.

Also, it should be noted that the various denominations have their special regulations governing their own ministers on matters of ethical conduct. It is the obligation of every minister to keep the moral law and to live as a Christian.

It should be mentioned, also, that the minister is supposed to be an arbiter in the field of morals and ethics; since he or she is personally regarded as a judge and diviner

12

in such matters, then it is the obligation of the pastor to engage in proper conduct. We should as soon expect—it might be argued—a medical association to draw up health rules for physicians or to issue a book on what medicine is good for a doctor, as to expect ministers to tell one another what courses of moral and ethical conduct are proper.

Last, but not least, it must be admitted that many of the matters involved are not of great importance. They have to do with jots and tittles and scarcely ever touch the inflexible bulwarks and buttresses of the moral law. When a matter does go over into a question of morals, then the minister's conscience, not to say the church, speaks up.

Nevertheless in spite of all this, there has gradually evolved through the years a strong consciousness of ministerial oneness, and this community has a definite feeling that it ought to be able to say something about the conduct of its own members. This growing ministerial solidarity may, of course, have its dangers. Henry Ward Beecher in his day thought so and decried the idea that the ministry should stick together as a unit. However, it is undeniable that an intangible, but powerful, professional consciousness has come to be felt among ministers today. As denominational walls have gone down, ministers of all groups and communions have felt themselves to be closer. The result has been that while the sanctions and findings of ministerial custom cannot be considered as binding on any person, they can be considered as advisory and suggestive to a high degree. While no code of ministerial ethics could ever be enforced by positive sanctions—nor should it be—the opinions and approved practices of one's ministerial peers must necessarily be regarded with great respect. Like international law, which gets its sanction from world opinion, ministerial ethical judgments must get theirs, not from an "interdenominational police force," but from the common sense of the ministry itself.

It has been clear for some time that there is a continuing

interest in and need for an up-to-date comprehensive outline of ministerial practices and professional ethical judgments. The various codes of ministerial ethics that have appeared have long testified to this need. This book, itself, originally published over fifty years ago, has served to focus attention on the fact that ministers do feel the need for a systematic treatment of the many personal and ethical problems connected with their life work. It has been revised again in answer to a demand that some of its statements and findings be brought up to date, that newer techniques and modern methods of managing certain situations that were not prominent a generation ago be properly dealt with, and that more detailed treatment be accorded certain situations in which a minister's professional service should be at its best.

In order to obtain more direct and empirical knowledge, and to obtain from ministers, themselves, a common mind regarding many points of professional procedure, before its present revision was published, eighty-six carefully selected ministers from over the nation were heard from and relied on as mentors and revisors of this book. Each represented a commanding pulpit, and many of them were nationally known. They were all pastors—with the possible exception of two or three, and these, themselves, were known to have had long pastoral experience. They were all persons who were regarded with respect as outstanding pastors not only by their own denominational family, but also by the entire populace in the regions in which each resides. Every part of the country and all major denominations are represented. Although the number called upon for this service was comparatively small, the quality of the people replying and the influence and the leadership that each exercised guarantee reliable and authoritative answers.

The response of these pastors was generous, and in many instances terse comment or advice gave additional insight

14

and help. Their replies were carefully collated, and the result is made known at the appropriate place in the following pages. Where there is a division of opinions or where practices differ, this too is noted.

In arranging the material, I have endeavored to give the most space to the most debatable questions and to make the work comprehensive while omitting the trite and dismissing with a bare mention the obvious. The general Christian consciousness has been drawn on for many sanctions where no definite authority could be cited. It was, of course, impossible to cover all relationships, just as it is impossible to classify all those relationships correctly by chapter and division, since this is an arbitrary matter.

A word may be said here about combining ministerial etiquette with ministerial ethics. Some who are impressed by the ethical demands of their profession are not always impressed by the need for the proper amenities of social procedure. They might, however, consider what was said by a wise old bishop once in addressing a group of his younger clergy on the importance "of little ways of gentleness that endear preachers to people":

> Although these things may not come up to the dignity of minor morals, I submit to you that this is one of the cases where it does well to tithe mint and anise and cumin. If by attention to these things we can make ourselves more useful, it is well worth while to attend to them. Of course a minister does not forfeit his soul because he does not know how to enter and leave a parlor; he has not committed a mortal sin because he cannot make a graceful bow; he has not offended against the Holy Ghost because he always wears a somber countenance instead of a smiling face. But if these things have so much to do with our success as ministers of Christ, I submit to you if our text (Rom. 16:1-15) teaches no other lesson but that of courtesy, it is well worth our learning.

It was said of a beloved English cleric that "when he went

up to the high altar, he made the garments of God honorable." The Christian minister today, whether conducting some impressive rite of the church or preaching the Word or ministering to the poor or, perhaps, helping in some menial task around the home, has the opportunity at all times to make honorable the high calling of God.

1

THE CHRISTIAN MINISTRY

By common consent, the Christian ministry is esteemed the noblest of the professions. Some may object to this classification, and some may wish it qualified by affirming that by the Christian ministry is meant a real ministry and not a counterfeit one. General consent, however, does give to the ministry primacy among the noble callings. Many ministers believe it to be higher in kind as well as degree, but they never press this upon others. They take the recognition of their "high calling," not as a mark of personal honor to themselves, but as an honor to that One who first called them. Like the Apostle, the best minister strives to apprehend that for which he was himself apprehended.

From the acknowledged truth that the ministry is the highest form of professional service spring several principles that form the axioms on which any consideration of the minister's conduct must be based:

1. *The minister must keep the nobility of the calling uppermost in his or her own mind.* Should the minister fail to do this, he or she had better take up some other form of

work. If for any cause the pastor begins to look down upon the profession or to feel that its glory has departed, then the calling is lost. The temptation may come, for instance, to measure the ministry by some of the standards that apply to the work of other professions—by temporal influence, by cultural values, by that ubiquitous and omnipresent measure of all things in our day and time, money. But should the minister attempt to use any of these things as a measure, failure will surely follow. The Christian ministry can no more be measured by these values than time can be measured by the mile or space by the pound. The professional standards of the ministry belong to another category, a spiritual one, nevertheless a very real one. Any effort to force a comparison to other professions will fail. The Christian minister must know this. The pastor who deprecates the calling in his or her own mind or who doubts its value is in a bad way. Let the story of Sir Lancelot and the lions be recalled. When, as Tennyson gives the story to us, the beasts rose up and each grasped the knight by a shoulder, a voice came, saying:

Doubt not, go forward; if thou doubt, the beasts
Will tear thee piecemeal.

So the minister who doubts the mission and work of the calling is in a fair way to be torn piecemeal between the twin lions of hopelessness and despair. The person who doubts not, but goes forward believing, will find the world believing also.

2. *The minister must hold high in outward acts the established reputation of the Christian ministry.* There is a degree of popular esteem in which the ministry is held, a popular regard, estimation, and measure, that is not the making of one generation, but of all generations. It is entirely possible for one minister to lower or injure this popular estimation. When this happens, a person's excuse may be that prevalent conceptions as to ministerial rights

and privileges are wrong, and, therefore, he or she is engaged in an attempt to set them right. Or one may say that new occasions teach new duties, and so on. But every minister should weigh very carefully his or her own thought and intent against the practice of the ages. Just as no reputable lawyer ever breaks the traditions of the ancient and honorable calling, just as no physician departs from, but holds in the highest respect, professional ethics and methods, so also the ministry should preserve and guard those traits which, by a common consent, belong to the highest type of ministerial service.

It would be impossible to list all the various ways ministers may lower the popular estimation in which their profession is held, but all know that it can be lowered. Perhaps ministers should have a custom such as prevails among Army officers. There is an old charge for which military and naval officers are court-martialed, known as *conduct unbecoming an officer and a gentleman.* What this conduct is cannot be specified beforehand—each case is brought to trial on its own merits. Sometimes it is for one thing, sometimes for another, occasionally even for unprecedented breaches in official bearing. On all such occasions, the officers themselves act as judges of this vague, intangible, but all-embracing law. Cannot the same standard be applied to the conduct of ministers?

For instance, in the name of "pulpit freedom" or of "necessary showmanship," some ministers have, frankly, become publicity seekers. The minister who thus breaks a thousand years of pulpit tradition (and this can be done in a thousand ways) may receive "two columns" notice in all the papers and be flattered as one "free from ancient shackles"; but wisdom tells us to await the final fruits of this person's life and acts. This is not to plead for a narrow-grooved ministry, nor for conformity to tradition-alism as such. One may be suspicious though of the minister who is so anxious to show himself "free" that he wears the clothes of a clown in order not to be taken for a "person of the cloth," or who turns the pulpit into a vaudeville stage to show that no bondage of pulpit is formal binding. Such ministers more often than not give the impression that they are lovers of publicity more than lovers of God, more anxious to proclaim themselves than their Lord. Buffoonery has no place in the pulpit of God. Care should be taken by each minister that public and private conduct not be unbecoming of the best traditions of the profession.

Conduct *unbecoming an officer and a gentleman* is always conduct unbecoming a minister, but sometimes conduct not unbecoming in others may be so in the minister. Henry Wilder Foote, in his book, now long out of print, *The Minister and His Parish*, observed that the community expects a closer adherence to moral standards on the part of the minister than from the ordinary man; there are "courses of conduct which, while all right for others, are unbecoming in him." This is quite true. A different ethical sense governs the minister from that which the ordinary person recognizes. A minister may rebel, and with good logic, too, at the implications of this statement. He or she may affirm that ministers have a perfect right to do what any other Christian has the right to do—theoretically they have. *Practically,* however, as Lloyd C. Douglas expressed it, people will make a priest out of a minister whether he or she likes it. The minister will discover that he or she is bound *not only by the law of the officer and the gentleman,* but also by something more, which may be called by various names.

The scriptural term *expediency* probably best describes this principle, which, while not always binding on others, must always be considered by the minister. Paul expressed this concerning his own Christian right: "All things are lawful for me, but not all things are helpful" (I Cor. 6:12). We need not push into the Apostle's deeper meaning here, but the successful pastor is going to learn that while certain

20

customs, habits, manners, and viewpoints may be logical, sane, and correct, it will not always be expedient to thrust them forward as such. Not that principles must be toned down, or that expediency itself may not sometimes be made an excuse for moral cowardice and compromise, but it is true that things that for others may be lawful, may for the minister not be expedient.

For instance, a certain minister was a great smoker of tobacco. After service one Sunday evening, he walked home with one of his elders. As the pair approached the house, the layman turned to his pastor and said: "Reverend N——, if you will not be offended at my request, I am going to ask that you do not let my boys see you smoking. They admire you very much, and I do not wish them to be influenced by your example and, while they are young, learn the use of tobacco." Now the pastor might have entered upon a strong argument in defense of his right to smoke and might perhaps have proved his case. He might have gone into a dissertation upon tobacco as something lawful, if lawfully used. He might even have made a matter of principle of it and said that he felt it right to stand fast in the liberty in which he had been made free and that he could not afford to give away his Christian liberty and that of others by yielding in this regard. As a matter of fact, he said nothing, but did as he was asked. He threw away his cigar and "quit" from then on. He said later that if he had any habit that prevented him from exerting the best sort of influence over the young people of his church, that habit was wrong—and his statement was right.

So it is with many points of conduct. It is perfectly lawful for a minister to associate with a social group that has nothing in common with the congregation, but the time may come when he or she will find that it was not expedient. It is, perhaps, lawful for the minister to tell the loudest and best jokes at the Sunday dinner table, but when that person again stands in the pulpit and reads the "watch and be sober" phrases that were written, not at a Roman banquet, but in the lurid glow of fiery persecution, throwing its shadows against an eternal background, the pastor is going to find that it was not quite expedient to tell those jokes.

In the attempt to be good mixers some ministers have used expressions and even told off-color stories that they hoped would prove them to be "like others." They little realize what they lose by doing this even in the estimation of those whom they would impress. Dr. Foote had it right: Whether we like it or not, the people demand a higher standard from the minister than from the ordinary person.

3. *The minister must never forget that he or she is one who serves* and must be on guard against any temptation the profession presents. The minister occupies a position in the local church and congregation and is placed on a pedestal in the minds of the people. Everything serves to dramatize the centrality of pastor, preacher, and executive; long continued and unchallenged leadership often intensifies this pre-eminence. The pastor's opinions in the official church meetings are quite often listened to by able business leaders as though an oracle were pronounced, and the smallest wish is sometimes regarded as something divinely ordered. It is no wonder that persons in the ministry, if they are not careful, will tend to think more highly of themselves than they ought to think (and there have been instances in which successful ministers delivered their personal opinions and judgments with an assurance of complete infallibility). Ministers' spouses often perceive this magisterial attitude on the part of their spouses before the persons are aware of it. Every minister ought, of course, to lead, but this leadership should be tempered with a deep-seated awareness of his or her own fallibility. The minister should never forget what manner of person he or she is. A sense of humor and a plainspoken friend or two in the church will act as a saving remedy here, and while a minister should

take the work seriously, he or she should never take the self seriously. Every minister should be on guard against "pre-eminence setting in."

4. *The minister must never for reasons of personal safety desert the parish and people when some great, universal danger impends,* such as a hostile invasion, an epidemic, or a natural disaster. Happily, this situation seldom arises—has arisen only a few times in our own land—but the unanimous voice of ministers of all the ages has declared that the pastor may not leave the people and fly to safety when the people themselves are in danger. The minister may send his or her family to safety or protection when possible; indeed, in visiting those with contagious diseases, the pastor must be extraordinarily careful to protect his or her home, but for the pastor there must be faithfulness unto death. It is in times of natural disaster, floods, epidemics, earthquakes, and bloodshed that the pastor may prove a tower of strength to the flock. If the captain of the ship is the last person to step into the lifeboat; if the airline pilot makes it the first consideration to save the plane, surely ministers of Christ can stay at their posts during times that try their people's souls, giving comfort and help and rescue.

This question was discussed at great length in Possidius' *Life of Saint Augustine.* It seems that the barbarians were laying waste all North Africa and were advancing to besiege Hippo. The ministers, with others, were deserting the churches and fleeing before them. Augustine, Bishop of Hippo, was asked by many priests what course they should pursue. They were not cowards, but doubted the wisdom of remaining and giving their lives for a problematical good. Many persons had fled, though some refused to leave. Augustine, the great church father, sat down and wrote a letter about it. It is solid Latin (and Augustine could write some of the most involved, as well as some of the clearest, Latin ever composed by mortal man), but out of the language of a bygone age a mighty spirit and a great man makes himself entirely clear. It is not right, said Augustine, to close the churches; it is not right for the shepherd to flee when the flock is to be left—the priest of God must stay! Today the universal voice of the Christian ministry says Augustine was right.

One of the distinguished authorities relied upon by this book insists that the rule against the pastor's deserting the people in time of peril or emergency applies also to a minister's leaving a local church in what may be for it a time of crisis. When some large building enterprise or heavy financial plan has been undertaken (especially at the request of the pastor), or when a fire or other disaster has struck heavily at a congregation's resources, no pastor should at such a time pack up and take a pulpit elsewhere. That there is validity in this assertion is, of course, granted; but it would be difficult to maintain that no pastor should ever leave a church or accept a call to another pulpit as long as the church is in difficulties. Most churches have problems of various sorts arising continually, and the church without difficulties has yet to be discovered. Circumstances here as elsewhere would seem to govern in this matter—the degree of involvement or the progress made in some pending plan as well as the pastor's responsibility for leading the church into it. No minister worthy of the name, after persuading parishioners to undertake some heavy financial burden or leading them to commit themselves to some momentous plan, would then feel free to leave these parishioners immediately upon receiving a call to greener, and less oppressive, pastures. Such moves have been made, of course, and may be made again, in the working out of the ministerial system. But many a minister has spoiled his or her record in a place by the manner of leaving it, and the minister who must follow such a person will have a much heavier task, thanks (or no thanks) to the predecessor.

5. *The minister must utilize time properly.* Like other professions, the ministry is not a matter of eight working

hours with pay-and-a-half for overtime, but of life service. The minister, therefore, gives completely to the profession. Of course, this does not preclude days off, vacation periods, and so on, which belong to all professional people, but the minister should feel that the profession demands the very best. To engage for a certain part of time in other remunerative work would break into the usefulness of the calling. One would consider it a lowering of a legal profession should one learn that a certain lawyer acted as a security guard during part of the time or a letting down of the medical profession if one found that a physician in off hours acted as an accountant for a manufacturing concern. Not that these other occupations are not eminently worthy and fully as estimable as are the professions mentioned above, if engaged in honorably, as they should be—but professional people universally hold that their profession demands their all.

The ministry is often tempted to depart from this professional role. Salaries are sometimes inadequate, and in some places it becomes almost a necessity for the minister to help supplement the salary by engaging in other occupations. This is bad—bad for the minister, bad for the calling, and bad for the people. Where there is any other choice, this should not be done. However, the hard but unanswerable fact is that sometimes it must be done. But consequences take no thought of excuses. The preacher who is compelled to buy and sell on the side or to teach school for a remuneration will find that his or her ministerial standing suffers, no matter how good the reason. The minister will do well to avoid any work outside the ministry if at all possible.

6. *The minister should resist measuring the vocation by the salary involved.* It is the just pride of all the professions that they place service above profit, but no matter what may be the case with others, this rule should not be forgotten nor deviated from by the ministry. The whole matter of ministerial remuneration could be discussed at great length, and local and national economics, personal

abilities, and special regional and ecclesiastical customs and regulations are all involved. However, after all has been written or said, the rule cited above will stand unshaken. The laborer is worthy of his or her hire and must have it, but with the Christian ministry it is the vocation, and not the wages, which must be supreme.

As a corollary, it should be said that just as the minister should not measure his or her own services in terms of money, neither should he or she so measure that of any minister. The "grading" of other ministers by the size of their respective salaries is degrading to the whole profession.

Using the ministerial, or priestly, position to get financial gain for oneself has long been known as *simony*. Technically, simony is "the buying or selling of a church office or ecclesiastical preferment." This, of course, has always been despised. One who measures every bit of professional service by its monetary equivalent, or who thinks in terms of money, is not far removed from the one who would sell spiritual gifts for silver or gold.

There is a subtle form of ministerial danger in which some have become involved, though not as much in recent years as earlier in the century. This is the use of the pastoral position or ministerial standing as a means of influencing the financial transactions of others, notably one's church members. Sometimes the minister has gone into financial dealings for private gain. Some have bought and sold stock in certain concerns or have promoted and sold stock among their own members. In some cases, it is in real estate that these transactions take place, and ministers, after becoming involved themselves, draw their people in. Such proceedings rarely result in financial profit and *never* result in spiritual gain. Sometimes the loss is both financial and spiritual, then church and ministry both suffer. This temptation is usually brought to the minister by some interested person; the popular pastor is often sought out and invited to "get in" on a promising transaction. The minister is perhaps allowed a liberal premium or given a large block of the first shares of the new company. The pastor's influence is recognized, and the name will lend sanctity, though not always salvation, to the speculation. But let the minister beware. If trustful people under the care of their pastor follow and get hurt in a financial undertaking, that pastor will have to face a terrible judgment from his own conscience. The business of the minister is to lead people along spiritual lines, not to aid them in making money. Let the minister shun all such invitations.

More than seventy years ago, the distinguished Dr. Newell Dwight Hillis of Brooklyn made the mistake of engaging in certain timber speculations, which turned out badly for him and for some of his friends. Dr. Hillis confessed the whole matter to his congregation publicly and asked forbearance. This story is told here not to reflect upon this good and great minister, but to recall the magnificent statement he made at that time.

> For years I have had a growing conviction that a minister has no right to make money, and does his best work without it. . . . At best the longest life is short, all too short for the noblest of tasks, that of the Christian minister. Great is the influence of the law and medicine; wonderful is the task of the jurist and statesman; marvelous the power of the press; great also the opportunity of the merchant and manufacturer who feed and clothe the people; but nothing can be higher than the call to shepherd Christ's poor and weak, and happy the minister who has never interpreted his ministry in terms of intellect alone, or has never secularized his sacred calling, and who at the end of his life is able to say: Behold these are the sheep thou gavest me, and not one of them is lost. (*Literary Digest,* November 23, 1915)

These words should be taken to heart by every minister. Let all temptation to make money "on the side" be shunned. The minister's responsibility is to do the Father's will. Remember that in the division of land to the twelve tribes, as narrated in the Old Testament, the Levites got no share of land for a possession. "The Lord" was to be their inheritance. "The Lord said to Aaron, 'You shall have no inheritance in their land . . . I am your portion and your inheritance among the people of Israel' " (Num. 18:20).

7. *The minister must guard the use of his or her name.* The pastor should not give sanction or endorsement to those causes or movements that are questionable. Men and women of prominence, ministers among them, have often had reason to regret the fact that they permitted their names to be used on the letterhead of this, that, or the other supposedly charitable or benevolent organization. Quite often, the purpose and methods of these hastily organized associations are commendable, but other things, such as unsavory agents or questionable advertising methods, sometimes make the minister and the public person wish they had never heard of the organization that they have so openly and hastily endorsed. People of prominence are usually drawn into giving their names for use in such work by being assured that the purpose is beneficent and that the name is all they need give; no details of the work will fall on them. That is true; the name is all that is wanted—but how valuable that is!

After the Civil War, General Robert E. Lee was, of course, penniless, but his fame had gone far and wide. The story goes that he was sought by a certain powerful financial concern, which was organizing an insurance company and wished to have his name as the president of the concern. It was explained the ex-commander would have no actual duties at all, although a princely salary would be given him; what the company really wanted was his name. General Lee heard the men through and then said simply, "Gentlemen, I have nothing left but my name, and that is not for sale."

8. *A minister must not encroach upon the field of another*

profession. Fortunately, there is little danger of anything of this sort becoming widespread, though the great interest in pastoral psychology and its relationship to psychiatry and certain types of mental and moral involvement has drawn pastors and psychiatrists into overlapping territory in certain instances. Much more might be said regarding this, but it is sufficient to say that both the physician and the minister should know where the work of one stops and that of the other begins.

There have been a few instances in which the minister attempted to prescribe medicine for people's physical ills. However, even in the few cases in which the D.D. is also an M.D., let medical ethics be observed, if not ministerial, and the case left to the attending physician. Needless to say, any criticism of a doctor's treatment of a patient should not be indulged in by a minister. Some have made trouble for themselves by acting as self-constituted physicians or nurses. Of course, in emergencies, where medical attention of a simple sort is required, the minister, like any other person, will apply first aid and do what can be done.

9. *The minister must not debase the profession by becoming a "handy man" for all the members of the church.* One pastor was kind enough to assist certain families a few times with the use of his automobile. It soon became the usual thing for the people to call for him whenever someone had to be taken to the hospital in the nearby city or to visit the dentist there. Sometimes, he was telephoned and asked to meet some member of one of the families of the church coming in on an airline flight; it was explained that the family found it "inconvenient" to be there. Now "I serve" is the minister's motto, and no matter how humble the task, the minister ought to be willing to do it for the Master's sake. But the pastor who thus becomes a "hewer of wood and a drawer of water" for everyone will not only find life endlessly taxed along this line, but also his or her own standing as a proclaimer of gospel truth will become

obscured. Where there is need, of course, work must be done, no matter how menial, but the people should learn that there is a higher duty conferred upon the minister than to run all the errands for the community.

10. *The minister must hold professional service in such esteem so as to keep it from being dissipated in the maze of shallow channels of service, which open out in all directions today.* The pastor is visited, for instance, by a person who wishes to arrange for a cultural and educational program to be given in the community and for the school children. The minister is asked to take the lead in this. It is argued that the planned cultural affair will bring an enlarged vision to the community and to the children. It will teach new lessons, teach new ideals, and lay a wonderful foundation for spiritual growth. It will be a magnificent opportunity for the minister to be public-spirited and, at the same time, perform a ministry. Will the pastor, therefore, accept the responsibility for the success of the program?

All of the above is true, for the sake of argument, but why not ask the minister to teach school? That, too, is a good work, a noble work. What about selling good books or distributing high class magazines? These will build up knowledge among the people. Why not ask the pastor to go out and ride all night with the policeman and see that the law is properly respected and enforced? That is a vastly important work. In short, why not ask the pastor to do any and every good job that is to be done in the town or community? Why not? Simply because the minister is not called to any of these things, noble as they are. The minister is called to preach the unsearchable riches of Christ Jesus, and anything less than this comes of evil.

Let the pastor avoid all sidetracks that lead off the main highway. Let the minister confine all of his or her energies to the one great mission—and God will abundantly reward these efforts as one attempts to live out the high calling of Jesus Christ.

2

THE MINISTER AS A PERSON

A remarkable characteristic distinguishes the Christian ministry from every other profession. This characteristic was perhaps best stated in an address given by President Woodrow Wilson to a band of Christian workers and ministers in New York on one occasion. The President, declaring the thought and teaching of his own father along this line, said that the Christian minister must *be* something before he can *do* anything. That is, character and person are greater than work—or rather, the minister's work depends on personal character. This is not true of other professions. It does not matter as much what sort of character a lawyer may have; the jury looks at the facts and the evidence brought out in each particular case. It does not matter what sort of person a doctor is if he or she is a "good doctor." But the minister as a *person* stands above the work, the sermon, the all. The preaching is measured by what the people know of the person; the work is tested by the character shown. The minister may have the tongue of a Demosthenes and the executive ability of a Richelieu, but if he or she is not personally known to be a good servant of

Jesus Christ, neither oratory nor ability will be of any value.

This is an extremely important conception for every minister to have. President Wilson was right; his father, the old Presbyterian preacher of Staunton, had gotten to the bottom of things. After a minister has become what God will have him or her to be, then the minister will immediately do what God intends to be done.

So every preacher stands on the shoulders of the person he or she really is. The minister lives among the people, has public and private meetings with them, and is known and observed by all. There is no awesome seclusion to heighten the preacher's sense of dignity. Today's preacher has no control over mystic or awe-inspiring symbols, as had the priests of other times. The people see the pastor standing clear of all the wrappings of ministerial cloth. Therefore it has come to be that by so much his or her character is known, by that much is strength measured—for good or bad. Because the people know the pastor, they listen to the pastor, because they see the person as a neighbor; they respect the person as pastor. What the person does speaks louder than what is said. As expressed before, primarily he or she must *be* something.

Physical Life

A prime duty for every person is *proper care of the body.* The minister will preach only so long as the physical body is a functioning organism in this world. The pastor will preach well, or serve well, only when the body, the physical nexus of the soul and the universe, functions well. Thought along this line is too trite to follow, nor may we go into a discussion as to ways and means of "keeping fit," with side notes on "How to Prevent Preacher's Sore Throat" or "Why Ministers Burn Out at Fifty" or any of the matters involved in this question. That the minister owes some time and thought to his or her body is conceded by all, but the pity is that the minister will recognize the common sense of this statement, agree to the entire list of obligations that should be practiced in the line of recreation and exercise, and then straightway go and forget what manner of person he or she is. Too many ignore the whole physical basis of life and reap as a result collapse in middle life or are handicapped for their remaining years by some personal disability. The remedy here is to face this obligation squarely and, come what may, work out some plan whereby physical exercise is taken on a rigorous schedule.

A certain definite time for *rest and recreation* in connection with the ordinary routine of ministerial life and labor ought to be set aside deliberately; such is the prevailing opinion among ministers. Of course, every minister is ready to spend and be spent for the sake of the people. In extraordinary emergencies, the pastor will go without sleep or rest, not to mention recreation. However, one day a week should reasonably be set aside for relaxation and rest, as other professional workers should also do. Sunday is the preacher's hardest day; therefore, some other day must be the day of rest. Monday was formerly regarded as the minister's "day off," and many still choose it. But the majority of ministerial authorities now indicate that Monday is no longer the most popular professional rest day. Many choose Saturday; some take Tuesday; and quite a few combine Monday morning and Saturday afternoon into a sort of ministerial *sabbatismos*.

One distinguished minister states that he prefers to work steadily for three or four weeks at a time and then go away from his parish for two to four days in order to rest and refit himself for work again. This whole matter is one for the individual to settle according to personal needs, as many ministers insisted when questioned regarding it. A number of our authorities feel that the pursuit of some hobby, even at irregular intervals and with no daily recreational schedule, will often take the place of a regular "rest day." Of hobbies it may be said that while they tyrannize those who adopt them (and are often looked at askance by others), they do have a balancing effect on life as a whole. Also, many ministers take advantage of health clubs that have extended hours. A daily work-out in the early morning or late afternoon is proving beneficial to many.

One positive affirmation can be made about ministerial recreation: It should be entirely unlike the routine work of the week, or it will not serve as recreation. If mental labor and the study of books, the visiting of the sick and the comforting of those in trouble are a minister's life work, then beware of spending your leisure in writing articles or "paying helpful calls," even though these may be agreeable pastimes. The postman should not take a walk on his holiday, and the minister should not continue the usual routine to achieve the proper results. The golf course or the tennis court, the drive to isolated places, the aerobic class or workbench in the garage—at any place or in any way that suits, the minister should rejoice in the liberty needed for recreation.

The Monday morning *ministers' meeting* for a time came to be an institution in many places, but this no longer seems to enjoy the popularity it once had. Present-day ministers feel that such meetings are too much like a continuation of their own regimen, the programs too fixed and routine. Most authorities consulted state that they do not attend such gatherings. "They make me gloomy," are "seldom helpful," "a waste of time," certain prominent ministers comment.

Bishop Warren A. Candler, the frequently quoted Methodist bishop of Georgia years ago, was once asked if he attended the Monday morning preachers' meeting. "No," he said. "When I joined the church I promised to give up *worldly* amusements."

But there are others who find these meetings very helpful, and all agree that the fellowship they provide is desirable to a high degree. "A man should help make these meetings what they ought to be. It is unwise for the stronger ministers to get bored and cease to attend," writes one man who is among the "stronger" ministers himself. It is a truism that young ministers are more quickly integrated into the ministerial community by attending these meetings regularly than in any other way. The objective here would seem to be watchfulness on the part of ministerial associations to see that their programs offer true inspiration and fellowship, rather than a continuation of the regimen that has bound the minister all week. Heavy educational courses often tried by local ministerial associations destroy the spirit of freedom that should prevail. Ministers like to talk to each other and are profoundly interested in each other. To that extent, they very much enjoy getting together. Of course, there may be need for definite group action by ministerial associations, and it will sometimes be necessary to make a business session out of the ministers' meeting. As a rule, however, business sessions ought to be called for that definite purpose and not take up the fellowship hour of the members. The minister's day of rest should be just that. It will not always be so, of course, because funerals, deaths, sickness, and other duties that cannot be put off will press in upon the day of rest; nevertheless it is a worthy goal.

An *annual vacation period* is a necessity in present-day life, for the minister as well as for all other persons. This view was not generally held by the ministers a hundred years ago, some of whom argued that the devil never took a holiday, so why should they? But that school of thought has passed away—perhaps because its adherents followed their theory too closely. Ministers everywhere hold that vacation is not an attempt to flee duty, but to be all the more ready for duty. The Master's "Come . . . apart . . . and rest awhile" called his own away that they might equip themselves for service among the "still dews of quietness"and "calm of hills above." His modern disciples feel that for them, too, there should be occasional periods of calm in which they may "rest awhile."

The length of the annual vacation, as well as the type desired, varies among American ministers. The vast majority of the authorities furnishing data for this book stated that a month is the usual vacation period. Most ministers seem to feel that a month provides an equitable measure of time off, though many hold that six weeks or two months would be helpful. It should be said that many ministers who are given long vacations use part of this time quite definitely for ministerial work—planning sermons, catching up on needed reading, and the like.

Preaching in some other pulpit during the vacation may prove unwise, though quite often the opportunity for new fellowship and the nonburdensome work of preaching a familiar and well-tried message may give a certain reflex inspiration to the minister on its own account.

Certain ministers report that they manage to divide their vacation opportunities so that a Sunday and a week or ten days is available to them in the winter as well as a somewhat longer summer period. But one able authority advises definitely against dividing vacation time. "It is better as a rule to take the weeks of one's vacation together. In this way they have a cumulative power."

In all fairness, the matter of the length of a minister's vacation should be faced from the church's point of view as well as from that of the minister. Any church loses traction when its pastor is away from the congregation for many Sundays, and it always takes longer to pick up in the fall after a pastorless summer period. Futhermore, there has been increasing concern lately among loyal laypersons who feel that their church's program is practically at a standstill for the long summer period. This concern is accentuated, no doubt, because many members of the congregation may only have a two-week vacation themselves.

Mental Life

An essential ministerial duty is the *cultivation of the mind* and the corresponding improvement of professional and spiritual powers by application and study. Long ago, William G. T. Shedd said that the holiest men have been the most studious. Even John Wesley, who was jealous of every moment of time both for himself and his preachers, gave the strictest injunctions to his not always educated men as to the duty of studying and reading. Wesley insisted:

> Read the most useful books, and that regularly and constantly. Steadily spend all the morning in this employ, or, at least, five hours in four-and-twenty.
> "But I read only the Bible."
> Then you ought to teach others to read only the Bible, and, by parity of reason, to hear only the Bible: but if so, you need preach no more. . . . If you need no book but the Bible, you are got above St. Paul. He wanted others too . . . .
> "But I have no taste for reading."
> Contract a taste for it by use, or return to your trade.[1]

The artist has a "studio," the business executive an "office"; the preacher should have a *study.* Indeed, since early days that room in which the minister lives, or is supposed to live, with his or her books has been known by the title just given—the study. Today, to be sure, since the minister must often act as a business executive, many churches have frankly adopted the term "office" for the room in which the church staff functions. But for the place where the minister can have privacy and prepare for his or her own distinctive work, we prefer the old name and old ideal.

[1]"Minutes of Several Conversations Between the Rev. Mr. Wesley and Others, from the Year 1744 to 1789"; Question 32.

This may be a room in the parsonage, manse, or rectory if true quiet can be secured there. It may be a room in the church, and the larger churches usually provide a study as part of their equipment. However, due to the frequent calls and interruptions that come to the usual minister—especially when the minister is known to be at the church—many pastors secure needed privacy by seeking a more secluded room or retreat during their study hours. There they may be reached in case of an emergency by the few who know their whereabouts, but on normal mornings they find it wise to put themselves beyond the reach of the telephone or casual callers.

Ministers seldom have the opportunity to say much about the lighting and other appointments of the study the church provides for them. A light, cheerful room is, of course, preferable. "Don't let them give you a study with stained-glass windows in it," a bishop once advised his preachers, "or you will have a gloom cast over all your thinking. Get some light and air."

The chief *study faults* to be guarded against are too much specialized study, or a bookishness that may result in taking one out of touch with life and its realities, and, on the other hand—and this is the more common fault in our active ministerial life—too little study. This last is particularly a temptation of the present age, since the minister in many instances is expected to be more of a social engineer than a student, more the aggressive leader of a large congregation than a cloistered scholar. Let the bookish type give more to executive and pastoral work, and let every person study and read systematically in other fields than those which his or her special interest and training are inclined to follow. "Grooved thinking" results in grooved preaching and in emphasizing continuously one particular aspect of Christian truth to the exclusion of others. The preacher seldom realizes how typed he or she can become by following, even unconsciously, some one subject of particular interest.

Unfortunately, what the minister does not realize, the congregation soon does.

On the other hand the executive type of minister whose delight is in planning and promotion, and in the driving through of an activistic program, needs to take more time for the reading of books and the well-balanced study of the Christian ages. With all the activities and enterprises that a present-day minister is expected to carry on, there is yet in the minds of the people the feeling that the chief duty of a preacher is to preach. "How acceptable will a minister in your chuch be if he devotes the major portion of his time to preparing sermons?" asked Murray H. Leiffer, writing to over a thousand influential laymen. In his book *The Layman Looks at the Minister* he reports that 60 percent indicated that this emphasis would be desirable; 10 percent was indifferent, while 30 percent dissented. There was a strong lay condemnation of any minister who "fails to spend adequate time in his study."

Time and *system* must regulate ministerial habits of study as well as everything else. The morning hours are voted by all as best for close application and brain work, and most ministers agree that the early part of the morning provides the best time of all. However, the great majority assert that the *entire morning* should be kept free for study, if at all possible, though the time actually secured for this varies with different ministers. "Four hours, six days a week," proudly reports one successful pastor, who has earned a name for himself as an able administrator as well as an able preacher. The average time secured by the average minister is about three hours a day.

A large number of ministers state that they prefer night hours as their time for professional study, though with others this period is mentioned as the occasion when they engage in general or nonprofessional reading. General reading is of professional help, in that it keeps a person in touch with the thought of the day and with the thinking of the congregation, but the vast majority of present-day ministers confess that they have to "catch as catch can" on time for such reading.

A large and often cumbersome *ministerial library* was practically essential in earlier days, when the minister was isolated from library facilities and the cultural advantages now found in every town and city. Then the minister's study was the only place where he might arm himself for sermonic conquest, and he found it essential to have about him the books that actually were the tools of the trade. As a consequence there grew the large, well-furnished personal library. In fact, a minister felt himself to be judged—and perhaps he was—by the books that lined his shelves. But times have changed. While the need of study is today even more pressing than in former days, modern advantages allow a certain streamlining of the over-booked library. The minister now knows that no matter how much time and money are spent in building a home library, there will be no great trouble in finding access to the books needed in nearby places. Every town has a public library, and with radio and television there are cultural advantages even in isolated places. As a consequence, there has grown among ministers the idea of maintaining a "working library"—one that is adequate, but not cumbersome. It should be chosen carefully for use, and not be merely a collection of impressive-looking books; it should be usable and not simply ornamental. There is, of course, no objection to the gathering of books, as such, when these can be secured by people who love them—as most of us do—and there are basic books that every minister must own. But many good ministers affirm that for practical purposes there should be a quick turnover of the ephemeral book, with its place filled by another of its kind or by one of the volumes that are timeless in their proven value.

A working library will, of course, include the desk books—several Bible versions and commentaries. At arm's reach will be a lexicon, encyclopedias, books of classic devotion, besides a prayer book, a directory, a discipline, or whatever may be appropriate for one's own denomination. There are so many rich and helpful volumes with which a person may be surrounded. A study of the reading habits of ministers, published in *Publisher's Weekly* several years ago, brought out the fact that those with the heaviest duties bought and read the most books.

Spiritual Life and Duty

Absolutely primary to the calling and work is a minister's personal duty to cultivate his or her own spiritual life. Present-day ministers have discarded some of the techniques of the past, but in insisting on this transcendent duty, they are as one with Christians of all the ages. Ministers are instinctively more alert about this, since they recognize a powerful but subtle temptation that their very life presents to them: since they give all their time to the work of God, they may be excused from setting aside one special portion of it for the expression of personal allegiance. But a danger lies here. "They made me the keeper of the vineyards; but my own vineyard I have not kept," was the startling text with which a well-known American preacher addressed a gathering of his fellow ministers. And while many of them knew that the Song of Solomon from which he took this text was probably saying something other than what this preacher had made of it, they knew also that he was saying something that needed to be said directly to them.

A person's very familiarity with sacred things may breed, not contempt, but spiritual obtuseness. The Bible becomes a quarry out of which to dig texts, not a reservoir for personal spiritual refreshment; prayer is something done for others, not for oneself; the lives of the saints, the rich devotional writings of Thomas à Kempis, Lancelot Andrewes,

41

and the classics of the past become sermon material with which to stir others, not the heart throbs out of which life may be made. And we become—God forgive us—professional! The quiet hour, the prayer, the rigid discipline we should like to see carried on by others should be undertaken by the minister if he or she is to be a God-directed person.

Most present-day ministers indicate that they take the first hour of the morning for their own personal devotions. Practically all insist that the need here can only be met by an unbending purpose. "Be rigorous," urges one. "Work at it"; "Don't leave it to chance," insist others, while "disciplined prayer" and "a definite period invariably kept" sum up the advice of all. One of our authorities does confess that to him it never has been satisfactory to fix a special period for devotions, and another states that wherever she goes throughout the day she likes to feel it possible to withdraw within herself and commune with God. But all others insistently urge a special time and definite regimen of devotion. Besides prayer and scripture and manuals of devotion and the like, one minister suggests a return to the almost lost art of meditation. All agree that no one can have a fulfilling ministry unless the fountains of a personal spiritual life spring up anew each day.

Duties to Home and Family

Foremost among the duties of a minister are those owed to the home and family. This is universally conceded, but too often the minister's home is immolated upon the altar of his or her work. The pastor has a hard task, but the pastor's family often has a harder one. Of course, circumstances must again be taken into account in judging a possible conflict of duties here. There are times when an emergency in the home demands every thought of the wife/mother or husband/father; there are times when an

42

emergency in the church becomes so imperative that it takes precedence over all home duties; this will be admitted. What is not so easily remembered, however, is that a minister's relationship to his or her family is as high and sacred as that to the church.

Happily, there is usually no conflict here, but, on the contrary, a most beautiful interlocking of work and duties. The better the mother or father, the better the pastor; the better the guide for the children of others, the better the guide for one's own children. Conflicts, of course, occur and two situations in particular may cause difficulty.

First, the minister owes it to the family to make a living for them. If not, someone else—relatives or the community at large—will have to. The family will look to the minister to provide food and clothing. "If I can't make a living for my wife in the ministry, I will resign and work where I can," a minister once said. He was not thinking of a luxurious living, nor of life in terms of money. What he meant was that if he should ever be faced with the fact that his wife and children needed food and clothing that he could not supply as long as he served as pastor, in that hard case, the obligation of husband and father would temporarily supersede the obligation as pastor and preacher. There are many pastorates and many church members, but only one home. Many look to the minister as a spiritual provider, but only a definite few—and these few exceedingly precious— look to him or her as an earthly provider. Neither the minister nor the parsonage family measures life in terms of the monthly paycheck signed by the church treasurer, but no parent, minister or otherwise, can forget those who look to him or her for daily bread.

It might be added that while a minister may not be able to give the family wealth or luxury, the pastor can and should labor to make a comfortable, happy home. The record of the ministers of this nation along this line is a proud one. The high percentage of successful men and women who have come from homes of ministers speaks not only of necessities supplied, but also of industry, frugality, and a stimulating mental and spiritual atmosphere about the parsonage, rectory, or manse. In *Who's Who in American Universities and Colleges,* there are many sons and daughters of ministers.

Second, the family of the minister should not be made to serve as slaves of the church, nor should their home be used as a public convenience for the entire membership. "Don't let ministerial life and domestic life get mixed," Lloyd C. Douglas wisely counseled in *The Minister's Everyday Life.* The minister's family, like any other in the congregation, ought to take an active part in the work of the church and its several departments. However, to force the spouse into the position of assistant pastor and the children into becoming prodigies of childish ecclesiastical leadership is wrong. It is not fair to the family, and it spoils the church.

All things being equal, the family of the minister should have the same rights and privileges, duties, and obligations that belong to other Christian families. Of course, it is recognized that the family in the parsonage should be a model family—but so should every home circle be. The reputation that ministers' children bear either for good or for ill is usually not of their own making. They are credited as being much better than the ordinary run of children, until it is found that they are not; then they are accused of being much worse than they really are. But wisdom is justified of all her children—including those of ministers.

Several good books have been written about the *minister's spouse.* It is sufficient here to say to ministers, not primarily to their spouses, that no matter what role the congregation expects him or her to play, the minister very properly sees the spouse as *his* wife (or *her* husband) to love and to cherish, to protect and to support. The spouse married the minister, not a whole congregation—at least that is what he or she thought at the time of the wedding.

Many ministers receive a calling to the ministry after they have been married for some time, and the spouse may find it difficult to adjust to the time demands of the congregation. Couples should be very aware of the nurturing needed in a marriage and deliberately set time apart for just the two of them.

In the matter of church work, the minister's spouse may be expected to give what time and attention she or he can to helpful service, just as any other Christian layperson does. If there is unusual talent or ability, let it be used as any Christian should. The greatest and most successful pastors and preachers have usually been supported—not supplanted—by a spouse to whom they and the congregation were in debt in ways that can never be properly appreciated or known.

The Spouse of a Woman Minister

A new situation has come about within recent years, as there are a growing number of women ministers, and this calls for a new role for their spouses. It is a situation that faces many men in secular, as well as religious, life when their wives attain public leadership, and sometimes fame, by being in positions entirely independent of their husbands. An example is the royal family of Great Britain, in which Prince Philip, not being king, always stands a half pace beside and behind his wife, who is queen. Likewise, the prime minister of Great Britain is a woman, whose husband stands in her reflected glory, as does the husband of the woman who is now a member of the United States Supreme Court. Such men are proud of their wives and help support them all they can.

In the case of a woman minister's spouse, he must necessarily support his wife and play his part in the local church as a layman should in strong, supportive, non-ministerial work.

45

Quite often today both husband and wife are ordained ministers and may be called to serve together in a local parish. In this case, mutual responsibilities can and should be worked out agreeably, but firmly, ahead of time, as cooperative duties of any couple should be. It is important, however, that if one is to be the senior minister in such mutual churchly responsibilities, this should be definitely understood in advance by whatever authority, local church, or general church that stations them in their mutual work. Administratively, as well as personally, this is important for both the couple and the church.

Personal Finances

There is one inflexible duty the minister owes to family, to the profession, and to the church: He or she must be absolutely exact on money matters. "Financial looseness or irregularity cannot be tolerated," Washington Gladden observed long ago. "All the preaching a man may do will not atone for unpaid bills. He may have what is to him a good excuse, but in the eyes of the world there is no excuse for failure to pay debts."

In this connection, something may be added concerning extravagance, or incurring debts without the strong probability of paying them. Every person can make mistakes along this line, but the minister should be very careful about incurring any obligation that is unusually heavy.

In former days, a great many things were given to the minister, and he was often the recipient of goods and provisions in lieu of money as well as of the *ministerial discount.* The United States was then a rural, agrarian nation in which money was scarce and the minister, and the physician as well, was often paid "in kind." To "have something ready for the preacher" or to sell him goods at reduced rates became customary in early American life.

But those days are gone and "clergy discount," as a survey shows, is not the common practice that it was years ago and is unknown in many places. Nevertheless in almost every region there are stores and commercial establishments where the practice is continued. The question is what to do about it?

An influential number of ministers take the position that such favors really are a detriment to a minister's work. They argue that gratuities and discounts destroy self-respect and that the people who offer them have a tendency to feel that they have been relieved of deeper spiritual obligations. "Let the minister be paid a wage commensurate with his work and standing," observed one well-known clergyman. "Then he will neither need nor should he take such supposed favors."

An inquiry as to whether physicians in various sections of the country charge ministers for their professional services or make a nominal charge or no charge at all elicited the information that the custom in this regard varies with different physicians. Some charge full rates, while others will not hear of receiving anything from the minister. When the doctor is a member of the minister's church, this is usually the case, and there is often a tie between physician and pastor that transcends financial considerations. In fact, the spirit in which ministerial discount is given largely determines whether the minister should accept it. There are some courtesies offered in a way that they cannot be refused without offending. For example, when a splendid Maryland doctor declined to charge a minister for his services, the minister insisted rather unpleasantly on receiving a statement, as he "liked to pay his bills." The doctor answered quietly that he was not showing a favor to the minister personally, but to the calling he represented. He added that as a doctor he did not have the opportunity to serve God as the minister could, but that his medical service was an avenue that God opened to him and that it was his pleasure thus to serve. What minister could have done other than accept after that?

This generous attitude, even though it is passing, represents the other side of this debatable question of ministerial discount. When a favor is granted as a mark of honor and respect to the profession, the individual minister usually takes it as such, and not as a private favor. The minister is, after all, the recipient of favors and even gratuities because he or she *is* the minister. The current thought among ministers is that the ministerial profession should be paid like other professions and that there should be no more gratuities. On the whole, this is well, but something priceless may be lost when pastoral services are to be paid for entirely in terms of cash. The minister will then, of course, be more independent, but so will the people—and God help a church whose pastor is independent of the people and the people of the pastor.

On the other hand, where the pastor knows he or she will be the recipient of a special favor—that the physician will not charge, the store manager will provide the goods "at cost"—the self-respecting clergy is likely to go without medical service that another person would instantly summon and will avoid the store manager, lest it be seen as seeking a favor. This is a strong argument against receiving any gratuities and discounts.

In general, it would seem better, where no pastoral tie is involved, for the minister to pay the bills like any other person, if it can be done without offending. And when the physician makes no charge, thoughtful ministers see to it that the doctor in question is remembered by a substantial present on such occasions as Christmas or birthdays.

Unfortunately, it is true that there are some pastors who presume on the ministerial discount, on the free medical attention. One such minister can do more harm than all the others who quietly go to other stores rather than appear where they know they will be given a discount. But it is a sad fact that because ministers are often given considerations that others do not receive, some of them unconsciously get into the attitude of mind that expects these considerations. Such clergy show their disappointment—and talk of it—when no special favor is given them; when one *is* given, they take it simply as a matter of course. Some have grown old in this habit of mind, and it is bad, very bad.

What to do about *fees* offered the minister for certain services has proven even more troublesome than clergy discount. There is more variety of opinion and of practice among the clergy on the matter of fees than on almost anything else. As it is, the wedding fee, which has long been a traditional and welcome visitor to the parsonage or manse, seems destined to continue. Sixty-one of our authorities say they accept wedding fees; five report that they do not. Twenty-three will accept funeral fees; thirty-five will not, though in the matter of funeral fees there are all sorts of qualifying stipulations presented. Many ministers state that when they do accept funeral fees they put them in some special fund and let it be understood that such a course is being followed. Others affirm, and very properly, that where the minister has been put to personal expense in connection with a funeral, as in traveling to a distant place, it is entirely proper to accept remuneration for such expenses. Some call attention to the fact that people in deep sorrow may be hurt if their kindly meant enclosure is not taken. Many pastors' studies are lined with books purchased with money given after funerals. A note should be sent to the family, indicating their gift was used in this way.

Certain ministers state that they refuse to accept any fees, even wedding fees, from their own members. They say that their pastoral relationship to their members precludes such acceptance. They will, however, accept fees from outsiders; that is, from those who have no claim on them. On the other hand, there are ministers who say that they always refuse fees from outsiders lest they give the impression that ministerial service is something that can be bought with a price. This last group, however, is not a large one, and most ministers feel that where people have no real claim on the church, the minister may more readily accept from them any money that may be offered. Dr. Raymond Calkins, speaking of this whole matter, stated, "I feel that the higher ethics of the profession call for the declination of fees for personal use. If accepted, it should be made plain that they will be used for charity."

Summing up the consensus of ministerial judgment: wedding fees are to be accepted, but funeral fees are not to be accepted unless refusal makes for unpleasantness and embarrassment.

3

THE MINISTER AS A CITIZEN

We now come to an often debated question: the minister's relation to civic and national affairs. He or she is a citizen of the state, like any other American, and enjoys all the rights and privileges of citizenship; yet, since the minister is the representative of the spiritual kingdom, which is not of this world, a strange dual relationship is encountered. How much a citizen of the world? How much a priest of God?

It would be impossible, if not wrong, for the minister to refuse to face the implications of citizenship. The pastor is, in fact, one of the civic leaders. Along with the judge, the doctor, and the school teacher, the minister is in a position of influence on the local stage more than the ordinary citizen whose vocation does not place that person before the public. In addition to this, the minister is known as one who can make a speech, and so is called upon frequently for addresses outside the pulpit. In the local congregation, it is a privilege and duty to address a public audience every week. This in itself would be enough to make the pastor a force in the local community and more or less a leader in civic affairs.

Now comes the question of how large a part in local and national affairs the minister should take. If the pastor were seen as an ordinary person, the now complicated question of relation to public affairs would not exist. But whether the minister wishes it, by virtue of position he or she is not an ordinary citizen. Clergy utterances are not only given in public, but they are also seized upon by both the press and the people as weighty words. It is true that clergy, with the schoolteacher, the doctor, and others, stands on a local pedestal. But the minister's words are commonly taken as of far more importance than are the statements of these other local citizens. This is because the pastor is regarded as an ambassador of God, and all that is said or done in an attempt to become divested of this ministerial character and to appear as an ordinary citizen somehow fails. How, then, shall this combination person, this citizen-minister or minister-citizen, act? That is our question in this chapter.

Civic Service

The minister, representing the church, is often called upon for public addresses, public prayer, and so on, in civic and national assemblies. Secular programs often begin with an invocation and sometimes close with a benediction by a minister or rabbi. Our legislative assemblies are opened with a prayer by a chaplain, and so are some courts; the government provides for chaplains with the armed forces of the nation and in such places as prisons and hospitals. The minister who is placed in such a situation will find that the course of conduct governing these actions is somewhat different from the usual pulpit and parish procedure.

The minister should realize, first, that he or she is placed in public nonecclesiastical assemblies—for instance, to open a public gathering with prayer—by virtue of the fact this represents the entire religious community and not one special branch of it. Therefore, it is absolutely essential that every minister in these positions represent as best as possible the universal church of God. By no word or deed should the minister give even a faint suggestion of taking advantage of the occasion for sectarian purposes.

Rarely does a minister transgress this unwritten rule. The experienced minister is well aware of this general representative character and is proud to be the spokesperson of the universal church. The chaplain of the state senate or house, the chaplain of the prison, the military chaplain, never forgets the broadness of his or her service. If the truth be told, these chaplains usually "lean over backward" in order to be impartial. Stories came to us from the armed services, telling how Christian chaplains ministered to the dying Jewish soldiers in the name of a common God and how Jewish rabbis held up the cross before the eyes of the dying Roman Catholics.

When ministers are called upon for any public address, as on Thanksgiving Day, school commencement, or other occasions, they act in accordance with the principle just set forth. The themes are general, appropriate to the nature of the occasion. Needless to say, one could scarcely afford to take advantage of such a situation for any private or denominational reasons. A breach of faith here would backfire with disastrous results.

Invocations at Public Meetings

Ministers today are somewhat divided on the matter of responding to the many calls that come to them for *invocations* at civic banquets, luncheons, club meetings, and the like. Those who object state that such meetings are time-consuming, and the service the minister is asked to render is often viewed as a perfunctory formality. "The importance of such service is overrated," declares a popular pastor in the capital city of a great state, while a Midwestern minister says flatly, "If you are invited simply because people expect an invocation and there is no appreciation behind it—skip it."

But the majority of modern ministers see an opportunity here. They feel that even at the risk of losing time, invitations of any importance at all should be accepted. "The occasion must determine the decision," states a minister of wisdom and experience. "Smaller events warrant a courteous negative to save time." Most agree that there is an opportunity for a representative Christian service and that it is well to emphasize in civic life the old idea that the blessing of God is to be sought for any important undertaking or public convocation. "Accept the invitation if it is a respectable event," advises a distinguished Baptist leader. "You may do some good."

The stipulation just cited—"if it is a respectable event"—indicates a caution that must be observed whenever a minister is invited to have a place on a public program. Will the appearance on the program be in keeping with one's ministerial calling? Usually, of course, it will be, and any doubt at all can be cleared by understanding beforehand the exact nature of the occasion. The presence of the minister, and especially his or her participation in any public event, is viewed as an endorsement of whatever transpires. The cloth of the minister makes wonderful camouflage, and Mr. Worldly-Wiseman knows it.

The professional rule that under no circumstances may a minister renounce ministerial calling or Christian character must be carefully observed on all public occasions. In the attempt to be viewed as regular persons at civic club luncheons, there have been ministers whose stories and speeches were out of keeping with their profession. Such persons lose far more than they gain and are marked down more than they realize by the very people they are trying to impress.

Interfaith meetings sometimes put a Christian minister in

a position where the virtue of tolerance is in conflict with the definite affirmations of the calling. It was reported in Washington, when a great, official international gathering was being held, that the minister selected to open the assembly was cautioned against making the prayer a definitely Christian one and was requested not to close with the name of Jesus.

In response to the definite question: If asked to pray before an interfaith conference, but cautioned to omit the usual ascription, "in the name of Jesus," in order not to offend other religious groups, should the minister refuse the invitation or respect the request? Thirty-six of our ministerial authorities held that the request should be respected. Twenty-eight, on the other hand, believed the minister should refuse the invitation. One bold character said that he would do both, accept the invitation and "pray as a Christian." However, it would seem that the very nature of the Christian witness prevents the minister from renouncing the calling. If a person may not appear as a minister of Christ, then perhaps one should not appear at all.

When the issue becomes one of public prayer against entrenched social evil, there is no uncertainty. Public prayer as a forensic act has sometimes caused political repercussions, and every minister knows it. In one state legislature, the prayers of the chaplain caused objection among the opponents of the moral forces. He was finally visited by a committee and asked to be less explicit in his public petitions. At the same time, he was reminded that his position was a political one, that political forces could remove him as easily as they had selected him. One may imagine how a delegation of this sort would fare at the hands of an Amos or a Jeremiah, but we have no sure knowledge of what transpired in the above case. Again, it seems the part of Christian integrity to represent the Christian consciousness and only that, regardless of consequences.

If public prayer before any audience is a ceremonial formula and that only, then why waste time—to make it no worse—in imitation of an awful act? If it is what it pretends to be, then in God's name there can be no trifling.

Privileges of Citizenship

The minister has certain privileges, just as any other citizen. Clergy should register and comply with regulations enabling them to vote. The only dispute that may be waged with this idea is brought by the one who says that politics is so rotten that the ministry should have nothing to do with it. This is sometimes heard from pious eccentrics on the one hand and from political bosses, who are neither pious nor eccentric, on the other. Dr. Washington Gladden once said, in discussing the secularization of the pulpit, that there are two classes who cry out against it: those who hold that religion has nothing to do with the world and those who do not want to know what difference Christian applications may make in this field. These two classes are the only ones who object to the minister's right to the ballot, and one does well to ignore such objections and be a responsible citizen with the other citizens of this country.

Besides the positive privileges, such as the freedom to vote and the inalienable rights to life, property, and protection, that the minister enjoys with others, there are certain ministerial privileges recognized by the state. It may be well to mention these here. They may be termed negative privileges, since they are in the nature of immunities given the ministry by the civil power.

1. The minister is usually exempt from *jury duty*. This is an outgrowth of old English common law procedure, which looked upon the *clerici* as men of mercy and not of judgment. It may be recalled that when a state trial takes place in the English House of Lords, the bishops, who are the ecclesiastical peers, always file out before a vote is

taken, on the theory that the vote of the clergy must be for—certainly cannot be against—mercy. American practice follows English, and no minister in our land is required to serve on a jury, except in a very few states.

2. The minister is not summoned to *serve in the armed forces* in times of war. This is an exemption that Congress has always granted under its constitutional power to "raise armies and provide for the common defense." During the First World War, certain clergymen affirmed that exemption from military duty was a slight to the manhood of the ministry. However, no objection of that sort was raised during the wars fought since that time. Universal opinion, both clerical and lay, agrees that the state does well in refusing to put weapons of carnal warfare in the hands of the *called* of God. Even chaplains accepted by and serving with the armed forces are classed as noncombatants and are not issued weapons.

3. The state will not and cannot force the ministry to any *service that violates conscience*. It cannot compel a minister to marry a couple; it cannot compel clergy to testify in court, concerning confessions that may have been made in a counseling situation—with rare exceptions.

It will be seen in the above that there is a recognition accorded the minister by the state that is not given to the ordinary citizen. These privileges should be recognized as belonging to the sacred nature of the office and should be accepted accordingly. In turn, the minister should pay back the state with loyalty and service in a distinctive way.

Political and Social Questions

We now come to a critical and debatable question. What part should the church and ministers take in shaping the social and political life of the community? Should the pastor actively engage in any movement for social or political change that will be at odds with local interests and persons? Should the minister speak from the pulpit on such matters? Some ministers and denominations answer, "Under no circumstances." Others reply, "In case a moral issue is involved." Still others, "Yes—on all matters that affect the life of the church."

Much has been written along this line. Usually one's findings are colored by traditional views. The older, more conservative, clergy as a rule abhor the idea of using the church or pulpit in any short-lived (to them) political conflict. On the other hand, there are those who decry with scorn the minister who, leaving the issues of the living present, preaches on the sins of Abraham, Isaac, and Jacob, but never speaks against local city council tyranny or judicial partiality. In *The Wicket Gate,* Studdert-Kennedy says in his own vigorous style:

> If the Church is to be a Church indeed, and not a mere farce—and a peculiarly pernicious farce, a game of sentimental make-believe—she must be filled to overflowing with the fire of the ancient prophets for social righteousness, with the wrath and love of the Christ.

More and more there is a demand for the church to come to grips with present pressing problems, economic, social, political. The question is one of importance, and good people differ much in their opinions. Some never permit their ordered and stately worship to be interrupted by anything, no matter what social or political storm may be raging among the people. Others rush quickly into what are clearly partisan matters and thunder at local political conditions, at one party machine or the other. Quite often these clergy advocate from the pulpit cataclysmic measures, all under the sanction of religion. When, for instance, an industrial strike is on, such ministers take sides and preach on the strike, sometimes with violence and fury. As a consequence, they earn from one side high praise and from the other unqualified hate. Their apology, if they give one, is: The church should be a big factor in the life of today. Of what use is it, they say, to ignore the present pressing matters of nuclear warfare, human rights, hunger and the homeless, apartheid, and instead preach on hypothetical questions dead and done with these many centuries? Let the church speak and rebuke evil wherever it is. Thus she fulfills her mission and strives for righteousness.

When all is said, there is no absolute ruling that can be made. Conditions vary, and a speech or a sermon that might be imprudent from one minister may be the fulfilling of all righteousness when it comes from another. There are times when the minister of God must speak; let the political chips fall where they may. It is questionable, indeed, for a minister to use pulpit influence to get a person elected to a national office or for a TV evangelist to use his audience to promote his own presidential aspirations.

Careful inquiry indicates that the consensus of opinion among ministers of the Christian churches will fall in line with the following broad principles or guides for conduct.

1. No minister should in public speech or sermon take part *in partisan politics* as such. Clergy should vote, as has been said, and will no doubt have a very definite opinion on the matters at issue in every partisan election. But *as a minister* or *in the pulpit,* the pastor should not pronounce upon partisan questions. This same principle will cover procedures in all conflicts of a social and industrial sort when no moral principle is at stake.

Some ministers endeavor to excuse their participation in factional matters on the ground that they are not appearing as ministers, but as persons. They are citizens; therefore, they are acting as citizens and not as clergy. This is a distinction, however, that the average person cannot comprehend. If a layperson sees the Reverend Doctor _____ speaking, then it is the Reverend Doctor _____ being recognized, and all affirmations on the part of the

Reverend Doctor that he is now not the Reverend Doctor, but just plain John _____, saying what he thinks means nothing to the person in the street. The layperson feels that if someone were to toss a brick on top of plain John _____, then the Reverend Doctor _____ would feel it pretty sharply—and so he would.

A well-expressed protest against this type of reasoning was sent sixty years ago to Dr. Alexander Whyte, the distinguished preacher of Scotland. Dr. Whyte had spoken out warmly and strongly on the Irish question then agitating his nation, and the notoriety he obtained by so doing stirred the elders of his church to protest. Their reasoning is convincing and timeless in its implication:

> We think that he [Dr. Whyte] cannot take such a part without to a greater or less extent compromising the congregation; he cannot divest himself in public estimation of his representative character, or fail to do something towards clothing his personal political opinions with the authority which belongs to his office; and he has been invested with that character and office . . . for other objects and on other considerations than those of secular politics. No one would ever think of questioning your sacred right of individual opinion and of supporting that opinion by your vote, but we venture to submit to you that many considerations . . . point to the high expediency of our minister abstaining from identifying himself in so marked a manner as you have recently done with either side of any burning political controversy.

2. The minister not only has the right but also is obligated to speak on *purely moral questions,* in the pulpit or out of it, whatever the political or social implications. No one can disagree with that. The morals of the people, the tides of the time as they touch people's lives—on these the minister is the declared authority.

But how is one to know what is a moral issue? Moral questions sometimes have political implications, and political questions sometimes have moral implications. A moral issue may be involved only in a minor way in some tempest in a municipal teapot. A needed social reform may be the least of all the planks in a political platform, and perhaps even then may bear evidence of having been tacked on to "gain the church vote." The most morally untrustworthy persons may have made the greatest pledges and be the highest bidders for moral support. All these angles give one pause, and, as hinted before, the minister who is permitted to be drawn into such local issues will discover many strange bedfellows.

In this difficulty, it is a safe rule to learn the opinion and thought of other ministers and churches on the matter at issue. If the moral sentiment of a famous minister, of several of them, or of the vast majority of Christian people declares a paramount moral issue to be locked up in a social, economic, or political campaign, then the minister usually has a right to declare his or her moral sense of the matter. But a minister who undertakes to decide the rights and wrongs of great political and social movements alone, or who carries on single-handed and individual warfare, becomes an ecclesiastical guerrilla or private sniper carrying on unorganized warfare. This is not to say that the individual may not be right or that the firebrand is not sometimes necessary to start the conflagration. It is to emphasize the risk of setting oneself up as judge of all morals, arbiter of all rights and wrongs. Common sense says it is better to move with the organization and to be guided by the consensus of Christian thought.

3. When ministers speak or preach on burning moral questions as wound up in political or other alignments they must *thoroughly understand every phase* of the situation. It should be remembered that in so doing the minister is constituted as judge, jury, and, as far as possible, executioner. The town, the city, the nation that sits as a higher court is going to review the judgment. It will wish to

see the evidence on which the decision is based. What are the briefs, pro and con? Has the side adjudged wrong had a chance to present its case, if not in "open court," at least in public? What was the defense? The minister has publicly ruled in favor of the other side, and the world wants to know why. If a minister has based the decision on hearsay evidence, common report, or "what people say," he or she will need to watch for opposition.

New Ethical Problems

To the moral problems that have faced human beings in every generation, there have been added to our age certain new issues, which modern science and invention have brought to the front. Questions of nuclear involvement among the nations; the prolonging of life by medical means when to all extent life has really departed; bringing about births by artificial insemination or with surrogate mothers; laws pro or con governing abortion; of science, allowing human beings to operate in fields never dreamed of by past generations—these bring about and will continue to present many new challenges of what is right and wrong. Christians, including the ministry, are divided in mind as to how they should conduct themselves and what position they should take on all such problems.

It seems that the rule cited above about finding everything possible concerning moral involvement here should be kept in mind as well as determining the opinion of other ministers. One does need always to be guided by a prayerful, informed conscience and to follow what he or she sincerely feels God's will to be. Christians have been divided from one another from apostolic times on down and will no doubt continue to be so in this and future generations. But right, in the long run, sometimes even after decades have passed, has a powerful way of validating itself. At all times, it is good to know and learn all that one may about these debatable moral questions; then one may, with the greater grace and power, declare his or her sense of the matter.

In connection with this, there is a fault to which ministers are particularly prone; it might be discussed in other places, but it comes in here very naturally. The ministry as a class is given to uttering generalities in a way that is dangerous. No one answers the minister from the pew or subjects the running statements from the pulpit to careful scrutiny. Bishop Charles H. Brent has said:

> The sermon is, by established custom, a monologue which the preacher delivers without fear of contradiction or interruption. . . . If the preacher, who is now protected by laws prohibiting any interruption of divine service, were to expect the flow of his logic to be challenged or questioned, there would be fewer weak arguments and poorly constructed sermons.

If ministers had to face the opposition that a lawyer knows will meet the statements made in court, they would soon become much more conscientious in their assertions. When ministers, in preaching, say that "Barth says thus-and-so" or "Moltmann taught this-that-or-the-other," they will be greatly perplexed if some ardent listener arises and asks on what page of their respective works that statement may be found, or just where Moltmann uttered the remark quoted. The minister who writes for publication learns this lesson: generalities in writing cannot be used as they often are in speaking. In speech, the ordinary preacher is tempted to forget this and soar away in beautiful flights of oratory to heights overlooking the world—and some of the facts therein contained.

Hasty generalization is a serious fault anywhere, but nowhere is it more to be condemned, or more dangerous to the minister, than in a political fight. In preaching their ordinary sermons, clergy "get away" with sweeping assertions, but if one undertakes to tackle the evils of the city hall crowd with a few broad accusations or to tell the county about the "courthouse gang," one had better have in reserve indictments of specific instances. Generalizations will get nowhere here. Be well informed beforehand that when ministers undertake to fight long-entrenched political and social evil, they engage in a conflict where no quarter is asked or given. After the first gasp of surprise from the persons attacked, the ground will begin to shake underfoot. They are out to "get that preacher" by fair or foul means. Ministers naturally shrink from warfare of this sort, but sometimes it must be undertaken. When it is, the righteous forces are often surprised and comforted to find what a power Truth can be to combat evil. Although the devil fights with fire, it is marvelous how Right seems to be its own self-evidencing witness, its own champion.

In summary, then, partisan or purely party questions should be left alone, but entering a civic or national fight on the side of a moral question is not only right, but also obligatory of the minister. Clergy should be most certain that a moral issue is deeply involved, and to be certain, they should keep their eyes on the great righteous forces and tides of the people, not on the judgment of an isolated community. If the problem is complicated by local prejudices, personalities, old parties, and so on, let the minister take all this into account. Then if, after all, the minister decides that it is best to "go in," do it like Esther. Put on the best apparel—theological, ecclesiastical, political, and personal—and approach the most uncertain Ahasuerus of modern politics with the motto, "If I perish, I perish." Thus recklessness and quick speaking shall be done away with. But when all is said and done, it is a greater evil to stand idly by and see right defeated and wrong triumph than perhaps to emerge at length from conflict with armor battered and dented but "valiant for truth." For such a one, to paraphrase Bunyan, "all the trumpets will sound on the other side."

4

RELATIONSHIPS WITH OTHER MINISTERS

Relationships with professional ministers present problems in ethics and etiquette. In fact, in the codes of ministerial ethics that have been developed, the nucleus has been an attempt to clarify the relationship between members of the profession. "Ministerial ethics" to most ministers means the way they feel they should treat other ministers and, even more, the way they feel other persons in the ministry should treat them.

Henry Ward Beecher once asserted that it was not good for ministers to associate too much with one another, nor to develop a "class consciousness." Another clergyperson decried the way the professions, including the ministry, "flock together and see things in their own light." While this might indeed be dangerous if carried too far, the growth of a great conscious fellowship is a magnificent thing, especially when this fellowship is composed of men and women who are ministers of God. Why should not this fellowship be able to make rules for its own members? If lawyers are the sole judges of who may be disbarred from the practice of law, and if physicians have a code governing their relations with one another, why should not ministers recognize that they, too, have a fellowship that may well look to each of them for conformity to its ideals?

Ministers, of course, will not and should not yield on that principle that is at the heart of Protestantism: Every person must find in his or her own conscience the ultimate guide. A ministerial fellowship able to prescribe and enforce rules on all its members would destroy the very freedom in which each member of that group ought to stand. Nevertheless there is a suggestive value, a guiding value, in the attitudes and pronouncements of the ministerial fellowship itself, and nowhere is this stronger than at those points where ministers measure and evaluate the propriety of their conduct toward one another.

Duty to Predecessor

Always there is a predecessor, and always the successor owes much to him or her. In a notable address, "Ministerial Ethics," the Methodist Bishop Charles B. Galloway said:

> Much of our work is to reap where others have sown. Their sowing should have equal honor with our reaping. A circuit, station, or district may be served the full term without the earnest pastor's noting much fruit of his labor. Another comes whose mission is to gather the golden sheaves and whose joy it is to sing the harvest song. Though possibly much honored, credited with being a more successful workman, he really enjoys the fruit of another's planting. . . . The apostle Paul said: "Now he that planteth and watereth are one." *(Great Men and Great Movements)*

Most ministers agree that the best plan of work, when one first comes into a parish, is to study the predecessor's methods and plans and continue them as best one can. In the beginning, there should be no radical break with the established methods. Indeed, Bishop Galloway, in the address referred to above, made this injunction quite strong:

> He [the minister] should endeavor to carry out his predecessor's well-formed plans . . . a wise master builder must leave many proposed works uncompleted. They require time for their full development. . . . Nothing is more common than for a pastor's cherished enterprises to lose or lapse when he moves to another field. His successor doubts their wisdom, considers others more important, and, with a self-conceit that would be ludicrous if the results were not serious, haughtily declares: "I have my own plans; another's I never could follow."

At any rate, local self-government and customs ought never to be rapidly changed upon a new pastor's arrival. The new minister needs all the popularity possible during the first few weeks. It will do no good, and may cause harm, to inaugurate sweeping changes at once in order to let the people know that a new hand is at the helm. In a few weeks, when conditions are better known, when the "well-formed" plans are known from the "ill-formed" that belonged to the former administration, the new pastor can then get on with his or her own projects and guide the congregation into the best of everything.

It seems the part of modesty as well as of tact to refrain from telling a great deal of personal history, opinions, methods, and so on on one's first appearance in a new church. Let the people find out about their pastor for themselves. Facts for the benefit of local papers may be given, of course, but before the congregation it is best to take charge quietly and proceed to work. "Let not him that girds on his armor boast himself as he that puts it off" (I Kings 20:11 RSV), is an Old Testament reference that will apply here. Furthermore, there are always the curious who are out to look the new person over on his or her first appearance, and who, when they know all about him or her, will lapse into their usual state of religious lassitude. It will not hurt to keep this crowd guessing—and attending—a little longer, before they resume their natural positions.

Every pastor will find, on entering a new parish, that the *predecessor's special friends* must be dealt with. There are some people in every pastorate who will never feel as kindly toward a present pastor as they do a certain former one. They hold a previous pastor in memory as the best minister their church ever had. They will speak of that pastor's excellencies to each succeeding pastor and sigh with regret at his or her passing from their midst. They may be polite enough to add as an afterthought that, of course, they like their present pastor also, but that same present pastor well knows that he or she will never take the beloved predecessor's place in the hearts of certain individuals. It is well to be very kind and sympathetic with these and to remember the lover's advice and "praise a rival." Never for one moment should a minister become irked by the ceaseless praise of a former pastor as it is dinned in his or her ears by devoted friends. If it is done purposely to worry one, as in some cases, it is answered best by appearing not to notice it; if it is done naturally, it should be just as naturally entered into. "Depreciation of a predecessor's efficiency ought to be as rare as it is reprehensible," said Galloway.

A minister is sometimes irritated by the tactless persons who delight in telling that Reverend ———, the former minister, never did as the new pastor is doing. It is very tempting to tell these officious persons that they should look and see that the present pastor is not Reverend ———. The new schoolteacher can do this with a roomful of pupils, but the preacher should not. "Ministers have different plans," or "We are going to try this and see how it works"—such replies will usually assure goodwill at least from these persons.

Every minister discovers some persons who dislike the former pastor. As Galloway says:

Every man of positive convictions will have had some antagonisms. His style was not according to every taste. Some oversensitive ones felt themselves slighted. On his first pastoral round a preacher will discover that his predecessor had a blade that cut and a twanging bow that sent an arrow to the mark. He will hear criticisms favorable and unfavorable. Then and there he has an opportunity to display the true chivalrous brotherhood of the ministry. . . . He should remember . . . the very persons who discuss so freely his predecessor will give him a similar introduction to his successor.

This is true. It may be wise to take advantage of any revived interest people may show when the new pastor appears, but under no circumstances should they hear a single word to the discredit of the predecessor. A criticism of a former minister given to persons of this type will go much further than if told to others. They will be glad to pass it on as ministerial approval of their lukewarmness or antipathy.

When a *former pastor* returns for a visit to the previous parish, it is, of course, the duty of the incumbent minister to call on him or her at the earliest opportunity as a mark of courtesy. If he or she has returned to perform a marriage ceremony or to conduct a funeral, the local pastor will, of course, take the charitable position that the visitor was invited to come for such a duty and could scarcely refuse. Former pastors often feel that they must return when invited for such occasions, and the current minister should understand that no intrusion is intended.

If the contingency arises in which the visits of the predecessor are not casual or disinterested, trouble may be made. There is nothing that worries a minister more than for a former pastor to meddle with the affairs of his or her pastorate. This is a breach of etiquette on the part of the predecessor, of course, and will be dealt with later, but from the point of view of the current pastor, what is the proper course to take? The best method is to attempt to find out what motivates the interfering pastor. If it is earnest though ill-considered interest, it will not be hard to point out that the letters or visits are not what is best for the church. If it is a natural desire or inclination to meddle, and if all hints fail, then it may be necessary for the pastor to be perfectly frank with the interferer and let it be known in plain words that he or she is no longer in charge and that any visits are not welcomed.

Duty to a Successor

When a new minister comes to a parish, taking up duties and obligations with which he or she is not at all familiar, the pastor should instinctively turn to the person who can advise and help more than any other, the outgoing pastor. There is the realization that the new assignment holds the usual problems having to do with the interrelation of personalities; the usual civic and public questions; the usual plans, half-done, all-done, or undone. The outgoing minister is familiar with all plans and, furthermore, knows of many hidden though important matters that the incoming minister should be aware of. The rocks that line the ministerial channel are known to him or her but not to the successor. The unanimous voice of ministers everywhere, therefore, asserts that it is a prime duty of every outgoing pastor to meet with and advise the new pastor of local conditions.

The outgoing minister should be ready to give a broad survey of the field and its work. If time permits, details may be discussed. If it is possible to go over the entire membership of the church together, the incoming minister will be able to gain an insight into conditions, which will be of invaluable service to the future growth of the congregation. Every minister feels obligated to supply all this and other helpful information to a successor, but at the same time the pastor should be on guard for fear that it be seen as an attempt at directing future work. One may well advise and state methods previously followed, but the minister with tact will know how to make it clear that the situation is now entirely in the hands of the new minister.

Some of the older persons in the ministry have remarked that it is not wise for the outgoing minister to tell the new person every detail about the people of the church. What a minister does not know may not cause any hurt. Let every pastor experience things anew. A new pastor's ignorance will give him or her a good start toward solving many problems. This will allow the pastor to blissfully and ignorantly charge head-on into many tangled knots, composed of unregenerate personalities and general "orneriness" simply because he or she does not know what the predecessor knows, and everybody knows it isn't known. The new preacher should be told much, but not everything. Give the people a chance as well as the preacher.

Every minister should give the successor a good "send-off" with the people. To quote Galloway again:

> The character of the introduction and commendation which he gives will determine the welcome his sucessor receives and will have a potent influence upon the entire history of his pastorate. If doubts are expressed as to his ability or availability, if fears are intimated that he lacks at certain vital points or has some objectionable pecularities, if confidential predictions of failure are made "just to one or two very special and discreet friends," the brother comes with a mountain of prejudice to scale and silent but positive opposition to conquer. On the contrary, if he commends his virtues, applauds his abilities, tells of his fidelities, rejoices in his successes, and congratulates his old flock that they are to be under such competent and consecrated pastoral care, he comes with hearts to welcome him, spiritual sympathy to sustain him, and assured victory to cheer him.

Even when the departing minister is in the position of

being discredited or rejected, he or she should be Christianly disposed toward the successor. Just as every child deserves the right to be wellborn, so also every minister deserves the right to a good start in any new field.

It is usually conceded that in general it is better for the outgoing minister to leave both church and parish before the new person comes to take charge. A former pastor's presence should not be allowed to serve as the nucleus for the crystallizing regret of many friends. It is also best for the outgoing pastor to avoid the opening reception, if one is held.

Church property, church records, especially the parsonage, if there is one, should all be turned over in good condition. This is a right to be expected.

Above all, when a pastor leaves a charge, let him or her leave it. No minister should be constantly going back to gossip with friends or hear comments on the work of the successor. Great harm has been done in this way by some ministers. The outgoing pastor should get all personal items—books, the piano, the typewriter, the food processor, the garden hose—and should give all a good-by, making it as tearful as desired, but having loaded the moving van, don't look back! Although the successor may not admit it, the presence of the former pastor after that can be embarrassing to the new pastor. "Get out and stay out" is the injunction here.

The difficult question may arise as to how to proceed when an old parishioner, or an especially friendly family, may ask a former pastor to return and officiate at the wedding of a son or daughter or to conduct the funeral of some loved one. Such matters can usually be arranged best through the current pastor, if the family involved will take him or her into their confidence. The pastor will be glad to transmit the invitation to the desired minister and the latter, in turn, to respond. Unless the current pastor is an extremely touchy and jealous individual, he or she will be agreeable to any wishes the family may have; if not, let the confusion be on his or her own head. At any rate, the parishioners should proceed through their present pastor. If the pastor does not actually transmit the invitation, he or she should be aware of it. This is a courtesy due the current pastor, and the invited minister must know it if the people do not.

Sometimes the people do not understand this matter as well as do ministers. Perhaps they shrink from informing their present pastor that they prefer another minister to perform a daughter's marriage ceremony. The pastor "might be hurt" if not asked to officiate. Perhaps they do not like their pastor and do not see how it is any of his or her business whom they ask. So they go over the head of the current pastor and ask a ministerial service from their beloved former pastor, and this puts the former pastor in an embarrassing position. The minister cannot accept without offending the current minister; yet, cannot decline without offending the family or friend.

Under these circumstances, ministers of experience have stated that they write a tactful communication to the persons who have requested their services, expressing pleasure at the invitation, but mentioning that it is courteous to consult the local pastor and that he or she no doubt will be agreeable to their plans. It may be tactfully added that the present pastor should be given some part in the ceremony if possible.

Such a message generally gets the right results. When the actual occasion is at hand, if no provision has been made to recognize the local minister in the ceremonies, the minister in charge need feel no hesitancy in suggesting it.

Galloway felt that it was "positively reprehensible for an ex-pastor to take advantage of his personal attachments to secure the honor of officiating at marriages in his former charges." This may be admitted if the ex-pastor is the instigator of an invitation in a conscious way, but where it comes unasked and unsought he or she may be excused. The procedure in such a case has been outlined. Galloway also felt it wrong to hold on to a former pastorate through much correspondence.

In spite of all this, it ought to be said that the breaking of the pastoral tie is no light matter. Often the minister and the family make friends and form connections that transcend the pastoral tie and that only death may dissolve. For such friends, the home of the minister is always open and to these there can be a pouring out of the minister's soul, for with them can be discarded the outward wrappings that surround the calling and show them the inner self. And to the mutual glory of the minister and the friends, let it be said that more often than not these persons who know the minister best as a person follow him or her closest as a servant of God. It would give much pain and add nothing special to the glory of the church were such ties to be severed when the minister moves. In a tactful way, the minister will know how to continue as friend and yet cease to be pastor.

A Maryland woman who was a devoted church member accustomed to having her pastors often in her home, commented once on a total severance of the pastoral tie. "I know that you preachers say that when a pastor leaves he should leave," she said. "But we like our preachers, not simply as preachers, but often as close personal friends. Then when they leave," she went on, "and we hardly ever hear from them again, it really hurts." She had something valid there, and it is possible, as many a competent minister has proven, that one can keep in touch with old friends and at the same time in no wise intrude upon the rights of a present pastor.

Invitations to Other Churches

When a minister is invited by a group or society of another church to bring some message on a public occasion, or perhaps to occupy the pulpit in the absence of the pastor, he or she should always make sure that the invitation is known and approved by the preacher in charge. Some church organizations take it upon themselves to form their own programs without respect to the minister of the church. This may never bring any complications, but when an outside minister receives an invitation from such an organization, the person ought, before accepting, to make sure that the minister of the church to be visited is informed of the invitation. The pastor in charge may wish to be present on the occasion in question and officially welcome the visitor, if it is convenient. A pastor might be very properly indignant if it were found that another minister had been in the church or parish in an official and representative way without that pastor's being aware of it. It is possible that the pastor may be blamed by some for not being present to welcome the guest of the occasion. So in all cases such invitations had better be "developed" somewhat before being accepted and the suggestion tactfully advanced that the local pastor ought to know and signify approval before an outsider can wholeheartedly accept. An exception may be made in those cases where, through long-continued association and cooperation, neighboring pastors are so sure of each other and their people that when one is invited to the other's church it is taken for granted that his or her presence will be welcomed by the minister in charge.

There is an ethical procedure that ought to be followed by an outside minister in the matter of supplying another's pulpit, even when that is legally controlled by the congregation or some committee. When there is perfect goodwill between pastor and pulpit-supply committee, this matter never becomes acute, and when the pastor is absent, for instance, he or she is glad to have the pulpit supplied by whomever the congregation chooses. But in case a minister is invited, whose disagreement with the pastor is known to all, this presence can be construed in no other way than as a reflection on the pastor of the church. If the people object to their pastor, let them get rid of him or her in a constitutional manner; until they do, that person is their pastor and must be treated as such.

New and Visiting Ministers

When a person moves into a new community, the usual custom is that the first visit should be made by the local people. This is a courtesy that should be remembered by every pastor with regard to "new ministers" who move in to take over the pastorate of a sister denomination or by any visiting minister whose presence touches the life of the local people. Such visitors and new pastors have the right to expect this courtesy from the local ministry.

Inquiry, however, among our present-day ministers makes evident the fact that this amenity is not observed with any regularity. Asked the direct question as to whether on their arrival at their new parishes they were called on by the local ministers, such pastors replied almost unanimously, "Very seldom." Pastors indeed are busy, but should not be too preoccupied with their own work to greet a neighboring pastor hospitably.

When a minister is a visitor in a community, the local clergy have the pleasant duty of extending the courtesies that belong to visitors the world over. Lavish entertainment is neither expected nor desired by clergy when they are visiting, especially if they are on a regular preaching mission, but the fellowship of a modest meal together or the welcome calls of other ministers have often proved a mutual blessing as well as the fulfilling of the old law of hospitality. The major denominations, at their conventions and conferences, usually create a "committee on courtesies" in order to welcome visitors and to look after various amenities.

Duty to Ministers of Other Denominations

Fortunately, interchurch rivalry has died down with the passing years, and the stern denominationalism of an earlier age has all but disappeared. Many communities now have flourishing congregations of independent churches with no denominational ties. Nevertheless between local churches, especially in small towns, there is considerable head counting, comparing of local efforts, and striving for local prestige. "In a Competitive Pulpit" is the succinct title of an article by Walter Dudley Cavert, which continues to apply today, although written years ago. This article pointed out and protested the fact that often ministers are in competition with one another rather than with the evil they all should fight.

> He [the minister] is hired to produce visible tangible results for his particular congregation and often he cannot strengthen his own organization without detracting from the possibilities of the sister church across the road. . . . The minister is in a position hardly different from that of the business man who finds it impossible to increase his own trade without taking customers away from his rival on the opposite corner. He is always under the temptation of thinking in terms of his own personal advantage.

Unlovely rivalry and professional jealousy are indeed abominable, but there is sometimes a healthy provoking of one another to good works. In this day of economic struggle, it would not be good stewardship to maintain too many church buildings if the congregations are small. Consolidation of church forces where possible and cooperation at all times are principles always to be followed, but in actual fact there is usually a field wide enough for all. The harvest of the unchurched is as abundant as ever. Every Christian minister has a right to reach out and gather a congregation for the Master without interfering in any way with the work done by another pastor.

Proselyting the members of other churches is universally condemned by ministers of all denominations. As Galloway put it: "Our field is the world and not some other church; and our mission is to feed, not steal, sheep." This is absolute.

Occasionally, however, a member of one church seeks to join another. He or she may have married a member of the new church, may feel more at home there, or may have taken a dislike to the other pastor and wishes to cause injury by leaving the pastor's care. At any rate, he or she comes and asks to be allowed to join the other fellowship. What about it?

In all cases of this sort, it is a courtesy for the pastor to whom the applicant comes to confer with that pastor who is to be left. If the facts are clear, the other minister can be trusted to release the member, and if denominational law permits perhaps give him or her a certificate of transfer. At any rate, it is not ethical to receive a member of another church without informing the previous pastor of the action contemplated, and the best results are secured by a personal interview between pastors.

Ministers usually feel free to receive members of other churches when these come of their own accord after they have followed the procedure outlined above. But as Galloway has said:

> Sacred Church ties ought not to be severed except for the most solemn considerations of duty. And the only office of the pastor whose communion is sought is to instruct the inquirer, but never to unsettle faith nor encourage the coming. In my own pastoral experience I have in several instances advised the applicant to remain in his old Church home.

A minister will do well to learn just why the new member wishes to join. "Spite members," like spite marriages, do not last. The fact that a person was "hurt" by a former pastor is not an especially good reason for accepting a transfer of membership.

Every minister will at times have occasion to visit in the homes of the members of other denominations—sometimes social calls, sometimes business, sometimes sympathetic, as, for instance, after a death. Most ministers stumble into the wrong homes at times, and in small places each minister is often thrown in contact with the members of other churches. In all this, however, the earnest, straightforward minister never offends or attempts to usurp a rightful pastor's place. Neighboring ministers have a pastor sized up after a brief observation of work performed. Their measure is not made by the letter of the law, but by the spirit of it. They allow the pastor a great many liberties with their people when confidence is earned, but if the pastor is a "sheep stealer" the gates of friendship are soon closed.

In small places, *local conflicts* sometimes occur between denominations and churches in such things as times for special programs, meetings, and so on. Many of these conflicts may be eliminated by a local ministerial association or by mutual acquaintance with the program of each church. In small places, an unusual or well-advertised program at one church becomes a town affair and draws from the other churches. Each congregation is, of course, anxious to keep its own crowd, and ministers are human enough to feel that they must at least hold their own. Thus rivalry may arise in securing speakers or special music and once this starts it goes a long way before it stops. Fortunately the majority of preachers cooperate in local work and avoid anything that may cause jealousy. Where a conflict in special programs occurs, an explanation is usually given by the one responsible. So much for interdenominational law, which, like international law, must enforce itself by the sanction of public opinion.

It ought to be said, however, that ministers whose zeal and enthusiasm are greater than their judgment can upset a whole ring of local churches. If a pastor, the congregation, and the pastor's opinion are in every paper, while the bandwagon crowd follows and the town tells what a dynamo the pastor is, it may stir the ecclesiastical dust and cobwebs out of the other churches. But we have seen it stir a good many other things, also—including a sullen hostility. There are greater things in the world than publicity and energy.

The good opinion of other ministers is worth more in the long run than the applause of the crowd. Reality, at any rate, has a strange way of manifesting itself. When a person is found to be genuine, whatever the methods, others neither fear nor are jealous; they rejoice to have another worker for Christ in their community.

5

THE PASTORAL MINISTRY

"His gifts were that some should be . . . pastors" (Eph. 4:11 RSV). The apostle, the prophet, and the evangelist may outrank the pastor ecclesiastically, but the triumph remains in the hands of the one who goes in and out among the people, visiting the sick, binding up the broken-hearted, living the Life. So it has come to be observed in our own time, as in the long history of the Christian Church, that the pastor is able to take the control out of the hands of either prophet or evangelist if ever there be need—as there never should be.

The grade a person may receive as pastor will make up most of the ministerial average when final records are in. "Two-thirds pastoral ability and one-third preaching" was an old-fashioned measure of ministerial ability. That, however, was before the day of social service and executive work that now count so heavily in that final average. At any rate, to be a successful minister of God one must be primarily a pastor, and this should be both known and understood.

Pastoral Calling

A wise and experienced older clergyman once observed that next to knowing how to conduct the sacred offices of the church, the young ministers with whom he had talked had always wished to know how properly to make a pastoral call. Calling on people of diverse occupations, states of health, manner of life, and so on is a difficult task, and ministers have a tendency to shrink from the labor involved in it. It is not so much the time or physical effort required, but the tension, the constant outpouring of nervous energy, the studied effort to size up the situation in every home and treat it accordingly—all this is wearing on the people of the ministry.

To a certain extent, the old-fashioned type of pastoral call has been superseded. City pastorates are often large; rural parishioners are scattered, and it is manifestly impossible in some situations for one pastor to cover the entire membership. Were pastoral work and preaching the only obligations resting on a minister, one might very well devote full-time to these two duties. But the multiplicity of other tasks falling on the pastor has cut heavily into the time for visiting. Some of these responsibilities—committee work, group meetings, public and representative events—while they take needed time, may have a value in helping the minister to work closely with the people and so to tighten the pastoral bond. But it is well for the pastor to remember that his or her presence in an individual's home brings one in far more intimate contact with the people who live there than any amount of letter writing or committee work can do. People are hungry for one-on-one sharing together.

Asked the direct question as to whether they think pastoral calling is as important, less important, or more important than it used to be, half of the ministerial authorities questioned affirmed it is just as important as ever, while a third regard it as even more important. "The increasing impersonalizing of urban life" is given by one distinguished pastor as his reason for holding the latter view. Irrespective of any difference of opinion on this matter, all ministers unite in agreeing that pastoral calling ought to be done as much as is humanly possible.

The universal regret of modern ministers is that they cannot find time to do this part of their work thoroughly. A number of them, however, claim that they manage to visit all the homes of their people systematically and regularly. One energetic Baptist minister writes that he gets into every home in his church—he has over two thousand members—once every year. His calls are necessarily short, about ten minutes each, but he gets them made.

Practically most pastors state that they hold general systematic visitation as an ideal, but that emergencies in the membership, hospital calls, and visits to new people consume most of the time they can allot to calling. The size of the congregation is a determining factor. When a church is so large that no one person can carry on this phase of the work without constantly neglecting other important duties, some other procedure must be followed. Those members who have problems or who need special pastoral help are encouraged to seek out the pastor in person, while an associate pastor is often employed by large churches to share some of the work of visiting. Priority in all pastoral calling is, of course, given to the sick and bereaved, with visits of welcome to new people taking second place. The elderly and shut-ins are also on the preferred list. For the rest, the busy minister does all that is possible and when sinking into bed at night often remembers with chagrin another call that needed to be made. A good shepherd is constantly caring for the sheep.

Concerning the visits of an associate pastor or of professional lay workers or of visiting committees from the membership, it should be said that these often prove of great help. They cement the church together, make people feel that the church cares for them, and usually bring a blessing on their own account. But it should never be forgotten that the people do not consider that such visits are visits from their *pastor*. With Protestant people, no one minister ever takes the place of another. They like both the associate and the pastor, but in great trouble they want their pastor to hurry to them. Every minister should be aware of this desire of the congregation.

On the credit side, it should be remembered that pastoral visiting, in addition to its value to people and church, is vastly helpful to the pastor. Going in and out of the homes of the people takes time that might be given to reading and study, but it opens a very real book of life. By some indirect, but powerful, alchemy, the things a minister learns in visiting the members—conversational chitchat, personal aspirations, trivial home happenings—become transmuted into sermon material that can bless and help. Something is always added to a minister's preaching when pastoral visiting is steady and regular; something vital goes from it when the visiting ceases. A housegoing preacher not only makes a churchgoing people, but the pastor is enabled to gear messages to human needs as well.

It has been noticed more than once that when ministers who have become known as great preachers after a time accept some non-pulpit ministry, such as teaching in a theological school or becoming an executive in some important religious work, their preaching ability begins to lack something of their former immediacy of expression. The lack is vague and indefinable, but those who have been familiar with such a minister's preaching do sense a difference without knowing why.

Dr. Murray H. Leiffer, in his book *The Layman Looks at the Minister,* noted at some length the results of a questionnaire he had sent to a great number of competent laypeople, asking pertinent questions regarding their attitudes toward certain phases of ministerial work. Not surprisingly, he found that in dealing with the minister as pastor, the replies he received were in line with what has always been considered prime pastoral duties. Pastoral calling, in the minds of laypeople, "continues to be an integral part of the minister's professional responsibility. Not simply social calling but calling at those times and places where he can, with the great resources at his command, bring comfort or religious insight or courage in the face of trial."

Questioned as to what they thought of a minister calling laypeople at their places of business, general approval was given, though, as one layperson put it cogently and forcefully: "The call should be brief, and the minister should have sense enough to see when he is in the way."

The minister is cautioned by all to avoid showing *partiality* to any special group, class, or faction among the members, nor should visiting be confined to any definite group or neighborhood. This needs only to be mentioned to be approved. The good pastor, like the good parent or teacher, has no favorites. The pastor, of course, has special friends and congenial spirits and would be something else than human were this not so, but officially the pastor is careful to hold all people as equal and to serve them equally. Certain persons, of course, need the pastor's attention more than others, but these—the sick, the dying, the elderly—are from every social class and from every part of the parish. The usual pastor finds, too, that some persons in the congregation need more pastoral attention than others and, like the Good Shepherd, will often leave the ninety and nine and go out after the one who otherwise might be lost. This is understood, but to get the reputation of being a minister to the rich alone or to outcasts alone or to intellectuals alone or to any one special group is not good.

Apropos of partiality, a pastor should avoid making a difference in the way he or she greets people at the door of the church or when visitors, friends, or new people are passing by. The minister should not show greater pleasure at meeting one than another, dismissing one with detached impersonality only to greet the next with warmth and enthusiasm. People are much more sensitive at this point than is sometimes realized. One of the best-loved pastors of today, who enjoys a national reputation, has the happy faculty of making each person he greets feel that he or she is supremely important. No minister can be perfunctory with persons—the couple being married is at that moment the all-important couple, the new member being received into the church is the all-important member.

Should a pastor make a *professional* or a *social* call? Ministers revolt at the implications of either of these words. "Professional," in the sense of something perfunctory or stereotyped, is an abomination to sincere ministers. A visit that gives the impression that since it is a minister's business to talk this way, therefore, this is the way he or she talks, is worse than useless. On the other hand, a social call, one that seemingly disavows the deeper reasons for pastoral calling, that skims lightly over anything but an affable camaraderie, means very little. To be sure, a certain amount of easy conversation and the observance of social amenities is expected of the minister as of any other person, and especially in getting acquainted with new people one moves slowly until a rapport is achieved. Also, in homes where the pastor is well known and loved, the ease of assured friendship gives an opportunity for conversation on all sorts of matters of interest. But present-day ministers feel that the pastoral call should be made to count for something more than the mere cultivation of friendly relations and that it can be of tremendous value. The courteous pastor, also, often calls ahead to let the people know of the impending visit.

Quite a few approve of the principle that the pastoral call should be social, but religious conversation should not be avoided. Others, however, are more decisive and definitely steer the conversation into the channels of Christian thought. Still others go much further; they definitely take over as the spiritual adviser of the home and make the moments count toward a definite end. When this is done sincerely by a pastor who loves the people and is loved in turn, the finest sort of ministerial work may be accomplished. "I do not get to this home often," a pastor may say. "I may not be back for a long time. I have many others to look after. But while I am here I want to make the minutes count toward getting you and your family closer to God. Let's talk about it." What home could resist a sincere appeal like that or fail to respond with an equal sincerity?

Most ministers agree that every call is different, and situations govern procedures in each instance. It seems, however, that since pastoral calling is a part of the minister's work, there need be no more fear of becoming professional when making a call than there is when preaching a sermon. When the minister comes into a home, he or she is welcomed as the pastor. Everything, therefore, is in favor of acting naturally as the spiritual adviser and guide to the home, and the pastor ought to measure up to the privilege.

Should the pastor have *prayer* with each call? It depends. A few ministers state that their invariable rule is to have prayer regardless of circumstances, but the majority report that they leave this to the moment itself. Prayer, however, even with a single individual and in the midst of daily life, has a spiritual value all its own.

Laypeople want their minister to feel free to pray during a pastoral visit if the occasion warrants, but they dread the visit of the unimaginative pastor who believes it necessary to offer a lengthy prayer at the conclusion of each call. However, they also find it difficult to accept a minister who seldom prays during pastoral calls.

It would seem, therefore, that the minister should enter a

home with the idea that there will be a brief, helpful prayer before leaving unless conditions make praying inappropriate, rather than the negative attitude that there may be prayer if conditions demand it.

It would be impossible to outline or describe the different situations in which pastors find themselves when making pastoral calls. One general rule might, however, be suggested as a guide in this difficult matter: It should be the aim of the pastor to become a part of the home while calling, but at the same time to guard his or her own essential character.

That is to say, adaptation to each home and its atmosphere will give a person at once an open path to the hearts of the people. To feel that they "have known you always" is a high compliment that some ministers are able to wrest from a family on the first call. This means that they have instantly sensed and sized up the home and its residents and have come in as one of them. At the same time, the last part of the rule above cannot be too strongly insisted upon. The minister must not forego personal characteristics nor minimize the essential nature of the calling. The minister must be exactly who he or she is to be comfortable in these situations.

To put this in other words, there should be an ease of manner and approach to the most pretentious, as well as to the simplest, home. This ease of bearing creates a confidence and a trust almost at once. There is no one who arouses more uncertainty and uneasiness in us than the one who is uneasy. A pastor who is uncertain of his or her mission and the reception in any home, or who by an apologetic air comes nervously into a strange house will make mutual understanding very difficult. Simplicity in all situations is greatly desired. If one is in earnest, this is not hard to achieve. If the visiting pastor wishes to be a helpful friend to a poor family among the people, the members of that family will sense that genuine concern. If the pastor goes into the home of the rich with the idea that he or she has something for them that no one else may bring, they too will believe.

The other side of this rule should now be remembered. In neither the home of the poor or the rich should the pastor lose distinctive identity in order to secure an "approach." "Adaptation without losing essential character" is the rule. If anything must be broken, it must be the adaptation. Better to be unable to visit a home, better to be unwelcome or disliked in a home, than to forgo ministerial characteristics and be ignored as a spiritual representative. Pastoral visiting ends when a person is not really a pastor.

Office Calls

In large pastorates and in cities especially office calls have come to play a definite part in ministerial life. It is possible to take care of a certain amount of pastoral work in such a way; indeed, some ministers frankly encourage their people to come to visit them, rather than vice versa. Ministers have always been open to approach by their people, but with the rise of pastoral counseling and the difficulty of obtaining privacy in home interviews, ministers have evolved a system of office appointments similar to those of a doctor.

An office at the church rather than the minister's own private study is quite often set as the place in which such pastoral counseling may be given, but of course there must be absolute privacy in all such interviews. Persons in need of their pastor's advice and comfort often shrink from having it known that they are seeking it. Sometimes they hesitate to make an appointment through the church secretary, preferring to approach the minister directly. However, in large cities a certain impersonality and anonymity are taken for granted, and where regular and well-known office hours are kept by a pastor, most people are prepared to visit when they feel the need. But sensitive persons, often the very ones who need help most, hesitate to come openly to the church office. Then the minister must arrange a convenient time and place to see them.

A famous clergyman-psychiatrist of Baltimore, in addressing a group of ministers about this matter, stated that he had found it a good plan to be in a certain pew of his church at definite hours. In this fashion, he made it easy for those too timid to seek him otherwise. One prominent minister suggested a stroll through the woods or park as an opportune way for pastor and member to talk, especially if the member was responsive to the appeal of nature. This same authority also emphasized the value of putting the consultant at ease and, if the interview is in the study, sitting side by side in chairs rather than with the pastor behind the desk.

Sympathy and understanding are the qualities most called for, and very often the minister finds that listening is the best service.

It cannot be stressed too often that pastoral interviews and everything relating to them are to be kept absolutely secret by the minister. Any reference to such interviews— alluding publicly to what "one who visited me recently" said, or "a man came to see me once and told this story"—may illustrate a point, but will set the congregation to wondering of whom their pastor is speaking and will make them fearful of approaching the minister in confidence. Some excellent counselors have been remiss here and, thinking that they might disguise names and persons, have repeated confidences entrusted to them under the ministerial confessional.

A distinguished Episcopal clergyman, the rector of one of the famous churches of New York, enjoyed a reputation as a great pastor. A publisher once asked him to put into a book some of the remarkable pastoral experiences and life situations in which he had figured—stories that would be widely read and greatly appreciated—urging the fictitious names and disguised allusions would maintain privacy. "No," said the rector with firmness. "It cannot be done. No matter how I tried to disguise them, there are some who would know. I received these stories in confidence and they will die with me."

Ministers should at all times be careful in the matter of *light comment and idle gossip,* especially regarding persons and matters of local interest. But nowhere should one watch words more carefully than while making a series of pastoral calls. Words thoughtlessly spoken are often remembered and given surprising interpretations after the minister has gone. It should be remembered, too, that if snap judgments or prejudiced comments are thoughtlessly approved by the minister they may be able to quote him or her as their authority in all future references. Ministers should avoid any semblance of carrying details of family or neighborhood gossip.

Successful pastors also warn their colleagues against speaking in a disparaging way of anyone in the local church unless done for a worthy motive and in a very guarded way. Unless it is necessary, it should never be done, for indiscriminate comment on church personalities is deadly. The way Mrs. ——— holds her head when she sings in church may be perfectly ridiculous, but the wise minister knows better than to make a remark to that effect. The pastor may know some very amusing stories about Mr. & Mrs. ——— but should never recall them in front of other church members. The gift of humor is a great thing to possess but not at the expense of hurting an innocent person.

Relationships with the Opposite Sex

While the number of female clergy is growing every year, the preponderance of ministers in the United States is still male. The following advice to male clergy most certainly applies to women clergy as well when they are faced with situations that may be viewed as compromising or that question their integrity or calling as ministers of Jesus Christ.

Women make up a large proportion of the usual minister's flock, and the pastoral relationship with them is complicated by the fact they *are* women. For a long time, there was a natural shrinking on the part of ecclesiastical writers from discussing matters that pertain to sex in connection with church work, but we live in a day when we are anxious to see things just as they are, and we have been enlightened several times by front-page headlines announcing to the world that another minister has stumbled.

Ministers will visit women quite often in a pastoral capacity. The man who thinks he can get out of this is much mistaken. He will find young women and old women among his membership—sick and well, rich and poor, great and small. Even if he confines his visits to the sick alone, he will find that a large proportion of these will be women. This fact had better be understood beforehand by himself, by his wife, and by his people.

In an article on this subject, Henry H. Barstow once said it is a tactical error for a minister to devote too much of his ministry to women. "Men and young people sense it and make their own comments. He will never reach uninterested men and boys by specializing in women." However, we should say that whatever member needs the pastor should receive attention, regardless of sex or any other condition. Ideal ministers will hold all the people equal in their hearts. There is neither male nor female, bond nor free, Greek nor barbarian, in the kingdom of which they are made ministers.

The danger in ministerial service to women is not so much error on the minister's part—though there are doubtless foolish women in church as well as out, and there are weak brethren—but the causing of comment and gossip that would embarrass the minister's service. The merest nothing will start a scandal, and the sensible minister knows it and acts accordingly.

It has been advised that calls alone on young married women in the absence of the husband should be avoided. It is suggested that some other person accompany the minister, and this is a sensible procedure when calling on a woman in her home. Repeated calls on any one woman should be avoided, since these will give rise to talk. If long-term counseling is necessary it should be conducted in the minister's office. Anything that will cause gossip should be shunned.

When a woman is sick and in bed, the male minister should always be sure that someone else is with her when he calls. It is a good rule to find out beforehand if she cares to see him. Wise pastors usually try to have the nurse or attendant go before to arrange the room for the visit.

When a minister comes to be well known in a community, he need not be so vigilantly on guard against gossip as when he is a newcomer, but any imprudence should always be avoided. More than one minister has been careless and imprudent and has had cause to regret it.

Visiting the Sick

Visitation of the sick is universally conceded to be a prime pastoral duty and one which yields a rich harvest to the pastor conscientiously engaging in it. Nowhere is the minister more welcome or more eagerly awaited than in the sickroom. "The sick are always in," Dr. Clausen stated. After a time they begin to wonder why their pastor does not hurry around to see them.

As sick people are not, in the nature of the case, normal, so the pastor's visit to them cannot be exactly on a par with that made to a well person. As a general rule, the pastor visiting the sick should not give the impression that the situation is a very unheard-of thing or "make a fuss" over the patient. Of course, the facts should not be avoided. "Here is my friend or my church member, Mrs. Smith, and she is sick in bed, and I have come to see her"—that is a straight-out fact that the minister wants Mrs. Smith to know he or she knows. But to give Mrs. Smith the impression that a terrible and unusual experience is happening to her is not good. In such situations, the attitude of the doctor can be taken as a model by the minister. In the splendid address to young physicians, *"Aequinimitas,"* by the scholarly Dr. William Osler of Baltimore, the great surgeon, put in a plea for "imperturbability" on the part of the physician or surgeon.

> Imperturbability means coolness and presence of mind under all circumstances, calmness amid storm, clearness of judgment in moments of grave peril, immobility, impassiveness, or, to use an old and expressive word, *phlegm.* . . . The physician who has the misfortune to be without it, who betrays indecision and worry, and who shows that he is flustered and flurried in ordinary emergencies, loses rapidly the confidence of his patients.

If this is a good rule for *doctores medicae,* it applies equally well to *doctores theologiae.* A good doctor brings calmness and a sense of security by his or her very presence, and so should the representative of the Great Physician.

Do not stay long with the sick. James Elmer Russell gave sound instructions along this line: "One should be deliberate in entering a sickroom as if he were going to stay all day, but after a few minutes, and certainly before the patient is wearied, and the very sick weary quickly, he should go."

In Edmond Holt Babbitt's helpful little book *The*

Pastor's Pocket Manual for Hospital and Sickroom, there is a list of "ten harmful things" the minister should guard against when visiting the sick:

Never ask a patient what the sickness is.

Never sit or lean on the patient's bed. Avoid jarring the bed.

Do not set the patient against the physician or hospital. If there is inefficiency or injustice, go to the proper authorities.

Do not make hospital calls when you have a head cold.

Give no information about the diagnosis if you know it. It is not your business to tell the patient how sick he is or is not. Information about him will be given the patient by his physician.

Carrying information about patients from room to room belittles your profession.

Avoid carrying worries, problems, friction, tension, crises into the sickroom.

Never enter a patient's room when the door is closed without permission from the nurse on duty. A pastoral call may be needed, or it may be an impossibility. Some patients prefer to have their doors closed all the time.

Never argue with a patient. The purpose of an argument is to win over one's opponent; not to give light. If you disagree, then just disagree, and let it go at that.

Do not ask a new mother if she got what she wanted. It is important that she want what she got.

It is to be remembered when visiting the sick that the patient is the center of attention. One is often tempted to talk to others who may be present, as this is easier to do, but the sick, like the elderly, are hungry for personal attention and should be made to feel that they are more important than anyone else in the room. Centering the conversation on the sick will, itself, demand a short, rather than a long visit.

Do not stay too long at any one visit. Remember, there is

an art in leaving properly. This holds in the sickroom as well as in other places. Some pastors never master this art and either break away with a "thank-heaven-that's over" air, or they sit and sit and mention the fact that they are sorry, but it really is time to go and sit some more and finally drag themselves out as though apologizing for casting such a gloom over a room as to leave it. If it is time to go, say so and go.

In regard to prayer in the sickroom, the particular situation in each instance will be the guide. This is the rule that a large number of present-day ministers say they follow. However, a considerable percentage state that they always have prayer with the sick, following in this regard the wise advice of W. Mackintosh Mackay, in his book *The Disease and Remedy of Sin:*

> There is a temptation to-day to pretermit bedside intercessions. The minister is afraid lest prayer will terrify the sick man or destroy the natural flow of human intercourse. "Will not a cheerful conversation on secular matters be more helpful than a solemn prayer?" Sometimes, doubtless, it will, and a wise tactfulness must always be used in such cases. But, as a rule, the spiritual practitioner, when he enters a house, should remember that he is not there to perform the *part of an ordinary visitor, but comes to bring spiritual healing.*

It is best for the minister, instead of asking permission to pray, to suggest directly, "Let us have a word of prayer" or "I always like to have prayer with my people (or my friends)," and then proceed to pray. Patients who desire prayer will not always ask for it but will be disappointed if prayer is not made. Certain types of men are afraid that it will show lack of courage if they ask for prayer when they are sick, but they will be secretly pleased if their pastor or ministerial friend authoritatively takes over and asks the blessing of God upon them.

All sickroom prayers should be short. Some prayers for the sick were better unsaid; that is, before the sick themselves. For example, one good minister visited an old friend who was ill and before leaving, prayed for him. He informed the Lord in lugubrious tones that both of them were men living on "borrowed time," that their short and evil days in this vale of tears were fast drawing to an end. The result was much depression for the sick man and much wrath on the part of relatives who had spent weeks of steady cheerful effort to persuade the invalid that he would soon be well. If a postscript were added to this story, it would be to the effect that the relatives in question saw to it that the dear ministerial brother never again got a chance to pray with this old friend. A Christian prayer ought to reflect faith and hope, or there is something wrong with the pray-er.

There are certain *times for visiting the sick* that are more appropriate than others. For example, the evening before an operation always finds one in a rather solemn mood, especially if left alone in a hospital room. The catharsis through which the physicians put one in order to get ready for the operation is sometimes carried over into the mental state, and quite often one searches one's own mind and considers one's own life. The patient is not afraid exactly—the normal person we speak of—but is glad to see company or to take refuge in a strength not his or her own. The pastor, then, if he or she has kept up with the state of things, has a fine opportunity for a helpful visit.

Prayer on such occasions is sometimes more of a problem than in the ordinary sickroom. There must be nothing said or done to induce any additional fear of the ordeal to come. Such would defeat the very purpose of the whole visit and would be no help to the operation itself. Cheerfulness and confidence and hope—let these be reflected in words and bearing and in prayer also, if prayer seems appropriate.

Another good time to visit the sick is when they are about to be taken to the hospital. At other times, regular visiting is in order; that is, calls when one is sure the sick will be at leisure to receive. Convalescence is a slendid time, as company is then much appreciated and time hangs heavily.

When a minister first visits a hospital, if not beforehand acquainted with the authorities there, he or she should always take the occasion for introductions. This is especially true if one expects to pay constant visits within the walls of that particular institution. The physician in charge, the assistant, the head nurse, the interns—all should be known if constant visiting there is to be a practice. The rules of the hospital should be scrupulously regarded. Usually, the minister is permitted some latitude as to visiting hours, but this permission should come from the proper authorities and not be taken for granted. In major city hospitals, parking permits are often granted to ministers who will be visiting frequently.

It is important to report to the nurse in charge of the floor at every visit. Although the office may permit one to enter and has given out the information of where to find the patient, it is courteous to report to the nurse in charge before entering. She may be treating a patient in the room, or for other reasons may not wish a visitor. At any rate, she is in charge and her authority should be respected. Most people forget this courtesy, and the nurse is correspondingly flattered by the minister's particular knowledge of hospital amenities. She is apt to tell the convalescent patient, after the pastor has left, that she likes that kind of preacher. "Reverend ———— knows a lot and seems to be such a good minister." So hearts rule heads in hospitals as well as elsewhere.

In visiting a hospital, it is well to speak a word to all other patients who observe the visit. This would be impossible, of course, in large wards, but in semi-private rooms it is not hard to do and pleases the pastor's patient as well as the other patients.

In the case of contagious diseases, health authorities take charge of the matter of quarantine and have no hesitation in barring the pastor as well as anyone else. But there are times when the pastor can go anywhere and must sometimes decide whether the visit will jeopardize the health of others.

All ministers agree at this point. Wherever needed, one must go, but carrying contagion must be avoided. A minister who visits in a home in which a contagious disease is raging and then immediately goes into another home among children would receive small thanks from the latter family. The minister's own home also ought to be taken into consideration, because to endanger spouse or children would be just as bad as to jeopardize others.

When a person is known to be dying the pastor should visit as much as possible. The conversation should be such as becomes Christian people when faced with life's ultimate test. Let faith be strengthened; let hope be in the atmosphere and trust in the prayer. It does not always pay to talk of death except *in extremis* or at the insistent will of the dying. Prayer with the dying is a very delicate ordeal, and no rules can be made for it, but many ministers feel better satisfied when they have made a commendatory prayer over the departing.

Dr. Gladden, discussing the ethics of informing the dying of their true condition when they are ignorant of it, took the position that although it is a "hard question," the responsibility of the pastor may equal that of the doctor. It is difficult enough, whoever does it, and neither pastor nor physician is eager for the privilege. Dr. Russell held that the doctor, and not the minister, should be the one to reveal the situation to the dying.

Next to the sick, the elderly have a special hold on the pastor. We need do no more than mention this fact, but let it be emphasized here that *attention* is what older people want. They wish to be noticed; they wish to be made to feel that they are still a part of the world. Some pastors remember their elderly members with cards or with occasional remembrances, as well as short calls, and such pastors reap a hundredfold. It is not impossible that when our Lord calls to mind the sick who were visited, the naked who were clothed, and the hungry who were fed, he may also add: "I was aged, and you noticed me, old and infirm, and you paid attention to me." Old people, too, are among "the least of these."

Comforting the Bereaved

When death comes to a member or to a close relative of a member, good pastors go at once to the home affected. It may be that the minister had been there just a few minutes before, but now must return. Death serves as the "you will report at once" order. Of course, quite often a minister finds that the person most affected, or the one whom he or she calls to see, does not care to receive anyone, but good pastors make their presence known at the door and offer to do anything to help.

Some suggest that the matter of the funeral be tactfully taken up as soon as possible so that the pastor may plan accordingly. It would seem better, however, to let the whole matter of the funeral be managed through the funeral director or relatives. The pastor has no absolute knowledge, or at least may not always presume, that he or she will be called upon to officiate, though many times it will be so evident that it can be taken for granted. But in general, it is better for this to be worked out in private by the family, and the funeral director may then inform the pastor of their wishes. The ministry is called on to play many parts, it may be admitted, but let us leave to the funeral directors their own special work. A funeral is a cataclysmic event in any home, and although it may be arranged at an inconvenient hour, the pastor had best leave all other duties and give unlimited service to those who need it most.

After the funeral, the comfort of the pastor's presence is even more necessary than before. While the funeral itself is pending, an excitement, artificial but nevertheless sustaining, prevails in the bereaved home. But when all is over the silence of an aching void begins to bear upon human hearts. It is then that the minister of Jesus Christ can be a true person of consolation. Let him or her go back as soon as possible—the next day, many ministers advise. The sorrowing wife or father or sister will wish to talk of the great trouble. Let them talk. Most ministers would agree that anything resembling hysteria should be checked, but wisdom now consists in letting the heart have its say. The tears shed are a very necessary part of the grief process. If tears are not allowed, the time taken to recover from the loss can be many months or years. The minister's sympathetic attitude means more than words can tell. The visits should be repeated at longer and longer intervals, until time, the great healer, does its work.

Visiting Jails or Prisons

In the city prisons or large penal institutions, an official chaplain is usually in charge of the work among the prisoners. If for any reason another minister should visit any of the inmates, the chaplain, as well as the other authorities, should be consulted first. The previous suggestions on getting in touch with authorities at the hospital will hold true also when preparing to visit the jail. Prison rules and regulations are more strict than those of the hospital and will be better enforced. The minister should know and observe these regulations.

The minister visiting the prison has the traditional reputation as friend and counselor of the prisoner. The minister may become such a partisan of the accused that he or she is viewed with suspicion by the authorities. The minister is sometimes charged with a degree of sympathy, which discredits justice. In most instances, this is not true, but the prison visitor should be on guard against the accusation. People confined to prison, especially those convicted, stand in the eyes of the outside world as guilty of crime, and crime is sin. The minister's attitude here must show no compromise, though it must always manifest kindness and the desire to help.

Persons in prison are often possessed by a strange mental attitude, which causes them to blame everyone but themselves for their plight. The judge was unfair, the witnesses perjured themselves, the prosecutor was a fiend—and all society was in conspiracy against them. But spiritual redemption for them waits for the recognition and confession of their own faults, their own sin. It may take courage on the minister's part, and sometimes will require repeated visitation to make such a person realize this, but the truth cannot be ignored. "We suffer justly," said the penitent thief on the cross. So says every criminal, who, after breaking the laws of God and society, receives pardon from God but not from society. Indecision here by the pastor will do harm. Let the prison visitor remember it.

Many courts allow that *confessions* made to ministers and priests by prisoners are privileged communications. A minister, therefore, cannot be compelled to testify against his or her will, when the testimony on such matters would act against the prisoner. Such confessions are, of course, inviolable, as are all confessions and confidential statements made to a pastor by members, whether in jail or out.

Should a minister ever take advantage of a confession or a confidential statement for the purpose of helping the person who made it or to prevent what seems to be a wrong? This depends. Faith must be kept at all cost; if a minister makes a pledge of silence, for instance, and under that pledge receives the confession or confidence in question, the promise must be kept. At the same time, to receive a confession or make a pledge binding one's future course without ascertaining beforehand something of the nature of the matters in question is not wise. Unprecedented situations often arise, but the unanimous voice of Christians today affirms that evil may not be done that good shall come.

Good priests and ministers who receive confessions indicating that something further needs to be done if right is to prevail are, however, in a position to persuade the confessor to make the needed move. In certain instances, they may obtain his or her consent to speak or act on behalf of the prisoner. This has the double advantage of fulfilling a helpful spiritual service on the part of the minister and of allowing the prisoner to work out a personal moral release by decision and action. Also it is in a prisoner's favor with society if he or she makes a confession or attempts restitution without being coerced.

Charity and Appeals for Aid

To deal properly with the whole matter of public charity, from a pastor's standpoint, is somewhat difficult. When possible, work of this sort ought to be turned over to a social service committee of the church, unless the community has a well-organized system for carrying on such work. It was this very situation that called the diaconate into being in the early church, as the sixth chapter of Acts tells us. The ordinary minister will do well to take a tip from the apostles and escape the obligation of serving tables. The Διακονία τοῦ λογοῦ is the minister's special work. However, there are times when the pastor must act as the almoner of the church. If pastors endeavor to push this matter off on a lay committee, they may find that while many needy persons have no objection to a pastor's ministration along this line, they do shrink from having a committee of the church aware of their poverty and need. This, of course, chiefly concerns the better class of charity cases, who are in need but making a struggle. There is another class whose members do not care who knows this condition, just so they are benefited. The whole matter of charity requires special tact and skill. Where possible, the pastor does well to see that this is attended to by others who have a special talent for it.

One of our poorer, ne'er-do-well members is at the door and wants to *borrow* some money from us. What about it? Here, again, circumstances will govern, but all things being equal, which they are not, the business of lending money to parishioners should never be begun. If a loan is made to one member, there is no good reason why it should not be made to others, and the news that a preacher is able and willing to lend money gets around in a wireless but amazing way. This results in loss to the preacher and loss of the member. There is no person who so diligently avoids us as the one who owes us money. There will soon be an empty place in the congregation where the person who borrowed money from the pastor sat, and an equally empty place in the pastor's pocketbook. Most ministers can frankly and truthfully say, when they are thus approached, that they have no money to lend.

Of course, there are cases of need, genuine need. These the minister can usually arrange to meet with money from a special fund or through a church committee. Most ministers, too, quite often place money—their own money—in the hands of the poor. This is right, for there are times when by every law of God and society a minister must give. When this is the case, let it be a gift in the name of Christ. Let it not be called a "loan" unless this is necessary to secure its acceptance. Let it go as bread upon the waters in the work of God.

Ministers have long been considered easy marks for

fakes, frauds, and cons. However, their reputation along this line is not as "good" as it once was. Yet occasionally some stranger knocks at the minister's door and leaves him or her after a few minutes marveling at the fertility of the human brain. The story most commonly told is of a dying relative in a distant place and how the necessary fare to see the loved one is lacking (or partly lacking), followed by a request for a "loan" of the amount needed. Most ministers can supply other versions of this story, and some of the variations are compositions worthy of the great masters. A good way to test such a person is to ask about a minister in the town claimed as home, and if the stranger admits knowing such a minister, tell that person that you will wire or phone and if the local minister endorses the claim, it will be all right. Ministers hear some queer objections to giving this information—they don't want the town to know of their condition; they don't want to trouble the preacher. Needless to say, a genuine fake at this point is glad to *nolle pros* the matter and move on.

Of course, not all supplicants are frauds. In this day of so many homeless people, the needs are great. "Do not neglect to show hospitality to strangers," says the scripture, "for thereby some have entertained angels unawares" (Heb. 13:2). But one might wish to know the genuine trademark of the angels when one sees it and not have to threaten to telephone or telegraph to get a visa on the celestial credentials.

6

THE MINISTER AND THE CHURCH

A minister's ethical obligations toward the church can be separated into two main divisions: those relating to the denomination or church general, and those relating to the pulpit, parish, or church local.

Denominational Relationships

Ministers represent their own churches or denominations in the minds of all people. There has been quite a discussion regarding this representative character of the ministry. Clergy who find themselves out of sympathy with certain of the doctrines or methods of the denomination whose name they bear have rebelled against the idea that their own ministry should be circumscribed or directed by regulations laid down by others, even by the mind of their own church representatives. Much is heard of "freedom in the pulpit" and of "Christian liberty."

This entire situation can best be judged when one understands the exact status of the relationship every minister holds with his or her denomination.

Most ministers will agree that every minister has entered into some kind of covenant with the commissioning church or fellowship to which they belong. With some, this was by vows of ordination in which the minister agreed to follow a certain course of conduct and, perhaps, assented to a definite creed. With the less centralized denominations, the questions asked and the agreement made are not always so definite, but in nearly all Protestant denominations some sort of test or promise is exacted of every person who becomes a candidate for that particular ministry. This test or requirement is, of course, always known beforehand by the candidate, who, nevertheless, answers the questions to the satisfaction of the denomination or takes the required vows. When this is done, the denomination, through its committee, congregation, presbytery, bishop, or council licenses, ordains, or approves the candidate and sends him or her forth as one prepared to preach the doctrine and carry on the work belonging to its particular mission. The church, therefore, relies on the minister's promises, answers, or vows. Most denominations never again formally question their ministers. For the duration of a minister's life, the church relies on the obligation once taken or vows once made. This truth is not apparent at a casual glance, but is of supreme importance in viewing this problem. Every minister has promised or taken an oath of a certain course of conduct or discipline through which he or she became the representative of a particular denomination. The minister was not coerced and need not have made this oath, but of his own accord he offered himself, was taken at his word and promise, received a certain stamp of approval, and was admitted to that particular ministry. Forever after that, he is declared unto the world to be a duly accredited minister according to the doctrine, discipline, and polity of the church.

The church after this has the right to expect that the minister will either keep the vows and execute the promises or terminate the covenant or representative arrangement if it cannot, or will not, be kept. All churches make provision for such termination of the ministerial status. Either church or minister has a right to end the mutual agreement. The church has the inalienable right enjoyed by every sovereign corporate body from the Congress of the United States to the small-town debating society—namely, to act as judge of the qualifications of its own members. The minister also has the right to withdraw from any organization whose methods or beliefs cannot be endorsed by that minister. This right to sever a relationship, which must be allowed to both church and minister, is not unfair to either, but a safeguard to both. To hold otherwise would be to insist that a great body of believers support and keep as their representative one who is not *in esse* their representative or to take the equally intolerant attitude that a minister should continue to preach assent to doctrines to which his or her heart cannot subscribe. There is no more reason for asking a church to place in its pulpits a person whose teaching and beliefs are not in accord with its own than for asking Great Britain to let a Member of Congress from Missouri sit in Parliament. On the other hand, there is no more reason for a denomination to expect a minister to serve in its pulpits against his or her own convictions of right than there is for Congress to pass a law establishing a State religion and compelling all people to subscribe thereto. The way out is clear. Let an irksome partnership be dissolved. The church can then get for itself ministers who will agree to its beliefs or meet its tests; the minister may then seek a pulpit with some other fellowship to whose doctrines or lack of doctrines he or she may agree or, failing that, may gather those with similar beliefs and worship with them where he or she pleases. Henry Wilder Foote has a fine chapter on the liberty of the pulpit in *The Minister and His Parish*. He comes to the conclusion that the minister's liberty is bound by the law of that church to which he or she belongs. This, the vast number of ministerial authorities agree, is sound and sensible.

The question of *heterodoxy* is at times a troublesome one. A minister may be in agreement with his or her denomination on most or all essentials, but may have a private opinion regarding certain minor points—of doctrine, for instance. It is sometimes said that every person is a heretic at some point. It is true that all have personal theories or vagaries of thought or imagination, and doubtless there are minor points of belief in which every minister differs from the thought of his or her own church, perhaps even from that of the long line of Christian thinking. Should a minister, therefore, withdraw from the church or insist that such matters deserve the attention of all? Experienced ministers do not believe so. Minor opinions, even doubts of an inconsequential nature, are no part of a minister's message, nor do they injure the work. The rule, "Preach your *dos* and not your *doubts*," is sound. Most ministers, therefore, leave unsolved or perplexing problems out of their public message and fail to enlarge on any difference of interpretation or doctrine that they hold against the thought of their own fellowship. There is no more reason for a minister to withdraw from a denomination because of disagreements with it on some minor question of polity or doctrine than there is for a husband or wife to seek a divorce because one does not like the style of clothes the other insists on wearing.

Certainly too much discussion of minor points will not be expedient before the congregation. It is very unwise to plant in the minds of the people vague questions and a list of speculations concerning problems over which the best minds of the ages have been exercised. The cardinal doctrines of righteousness and truth are being violated daily, and there is need to preach *them*. Leave speculation alone, say the wisest of the ministers, and preach from the vast reservoir of truth that is filled to overflowing. "But avoid stupid controversies, genealogies, dissensions, and quarrels over the law, for they are unprofitable and futile" (Titus 3:9 RSV).

What is to most ministers a minor matter, unprofitable and vain, may become to one person or to many people a question of the highest importance. Such persons may believe that to keep silent is to do wrong. If the church will not see this matter in the light in which the minister views it, such a person may feel impelled to withdraw from its fellowship. This has happened numerous times, and there is no discredit to either church or minister when a spirit of fairness and toleration has been mutually manifested. The minister is the judge. If one does decide to withdraw of his or her own accord, formal notice should be given. Then in an orderly way, all papers, records, and property that have been held by virtue of the connection that is now terminated should be turned over to the proper authorities.

Criticism and disparaging remarks about one's own denomination are sometimes heard from the pulpit. Often this is done in the spirit of the family circle whose members feel that they have the right to criticize one another, since they love one another. However, it is not wise, nor will it always be understood, when members of either a family or a church publicly criticize their own. To say the least, it is in bad taste.

Legitimate and constructive criticism is, of course, looked for by every large organization, and these, including churches, usually have constitutional ways for registering the opinion of their own membership and for making any changes that may be deemed wise. Most ministers are profoundly interested in the general relationships of their own denomination and are enthusiastic observers of its courses of action. However, most of them consider it better to effect reforms or to obtain changes in policy or creed through constitutional methods. They do not usually go to such lengths as to damage the church by

111

public criticism or threatened withdrawal. Many of the ecclesiastical statesman type ignore such methods, nor do they issue many controversial statements to the general press. They wait until the time of the council or convention or assembly, and then before their peers in conference assembled make the fight for what they hold to be right. Criticism of the general polity of the church, when it comes from local pulpits, seldom does any good and is embarrassing to visitors.

Disagreement within the denomination may bring up the possibility of *schism*. The questions will be asked: What is to be done when no redress for wrong may be obtained through denominational channels? Is one then justified in using extraconstitutionl means to bring about what he or she believes to be right? Shall one neglect the "regular official channels" through which protests and requests are expected to pass from the lowest officer to the highest (provided no one stops them *en route*) and appeal directly to the powers that be, irrespective of constitutional methods or anything else?

This is the crucial question regarding all rebellion, all revolution. In a measure, each case is to be judged on its on merits and, historically and politically at least, by its results. Martin Luther and Martin Luther King, Jr., to name two notable examples, achieved what history declares to have been right by using extraconstitutional means. In the case of the ordinary minister and the laws of the church, most ministers are inclined to take the view that the dissenting person will, as a rule, better achieve results by working through regular channels than by disregarding them. Ministers who decide to gain their own ends, regardless of constitution or previous custom, although they may be right under other standards, must be prepared to be treated as rebels by the organization. It may be observed also that schismatic types as a rule seldom get very far. If they have truth with them, that will eventually prevail; however, if they have but a modicum of truth, they will prevail only in a moderate way. Neither churches nor political parties last long when founded on one issue, and the graveyard of dead churches and political parties will show it. One idea may create a schism, but will not produce an enduring church. In the last analysis, every idea must stand on its own strength and receive for itself what life it may.

As a rule, individuals get further by standing with their organization. People are intuitively doubtful about the person who bolts. There is usually a certain type in every organization that will rule or ruin and will not be bound by majority decision. Christian liberty should not be curtailed, nor that of conscience. The minister who decides to revolt may do so, but that person must be entirely willing to wear the stigma of a rebel.

Candidature and Overture

The whole matter of candidature and overture is of vast interest to ministers in all denominations, except those whose clergy are appointed rather than called to their respective pulpits. Washington Gladden, in his book *The Christian Pastor and the Working Church,* laid down some rules for candidature that present-day ministers agree are still valid. These may be discussed in a twofold way: the seeking of a pastorate by a minister and the efforts to obtain a minister by a "vacant" church.

It is agreed by all that a vacant church has the right to make overtures to whomever it pleases, whether the minister in question is attached or unattached, "as no church possesses exclusive right to any minister." It may be imagined, however, that complications and ill feelings may arise when one church is found endeavoring to take away the beloved minister of another congregation. A great deal depends on how the subject is broached and what sort of spirit is maintained. Present-day ministers agree that a minister should be passive in regard to such overtures, until of course it becomes his or her duty to make a decision. Certainly, the pastor who obviously has an ear to the ground to catch attractive calls from other places, or who takes pleasure in flaunting before his or her congregation flattering offers from other churches, will create the impression of being on the auction block for the highest bidder.

When overtures come to a minister from a church whose pastor has not yet resigned, the universal instruction of the ministry is to let such calls alone. This is absolute. Absolute also is the feeling of the majority of ministers that something more than "private inquiries" will be required before a person is justfied in assuming that a certain pulpit will be vacated. In fact, many ministers doubt that even a public announcement regarding a pulpit vacancy gives a person enough on which to proceed; the pastor should be fairly informed of the situation by interested parties among the church's members before formally consenting to have his or her name considered. But others feel that this is quibbling and that where there is an actual opening any minister may be allowed the right to see that his or her name is properly put before the seeking congregation.

Ministerial authorities also approve the unwritten rule that "no church should enter into negotiations with a second candidate while it has one before it whose case is not yet determined; and no minister should be considered as a candidate by a church until positively assured that that church is negotiating with no candidate with respect to whom it has not reached a decision." A minister, of course, may not have the power to forestall overtures from other churches, but the last part of the above quotation may be heeded. Ministers shrink from being drawn into a contest with one another for a vacant place and preserve self-respect better by refusing to strive with one another for an open pulpit.

When the pastor has not resigned and the pulpit is not vacant, no minister worthy of the name will listen to an overture or make one. The laws of the various denominations prescribe that, but there is another and greater law whose whole temper and spirit forbid a minister of God to force out, or conspire against, the deposition of another minister. Let no one be deceived. The excuse may be given to oneself, "I can do well the work of God that I see the incumbent doing so poorly." That may be true, but we must allow God to oversee his own work. Certainly, no one can possibly bring about good by doing ill.

Where a minister decides to seek a church that is vacant, it is agreed that he or she is at liberty to advance the candidacy by any aboveboard and dignified means. The majority of ministerial authorities consulted about this assert that it is better for the candidate not to apply in person, but to get some other person or friend to introduce the candidate and emphasize any qualifications. There are others who take what they consider a more realistic view, holding that aggressive methods may bring results in a more direct way.

The personality of the pastor is the decisive factor here, and neither commendatory letters nor hearsay praise will ever equal a ten-minute view of the person in question in the pulpit. On the other hand, what may be all right ethically may be a mistake tactically, and, as wise ministers sometimes say, it is better for the church to seek the pastor than for the pastor to seek the church. Ministers, therefore, as a rule protect against the idea of preaching trial sermons. They urge, and with truth, that a congregation seeking a new pastor should send a committee to the current church rather than extend an invitation to come to theirs. From both the minister's standpoint and that of the seeking church, this is the best procedure. The minister is presumably at home in a well-established pulpit and is not conscious of being tested by alien standards; the visiting group from the seeking congregation has the advantage of judging the preacher by what may be taken as a fair sample of a normal Sunday worship service. If nothing comes of it, there is no embarrassment on the part of either the committee or the minister.

There are, however, many instances in which this method of appraising a prospective pastor may not be possible. In such cases, trial sermons may not only be advisable but also necessary. Modern ministers are realistic enough to agree to this, though one writes that there must be no "contest," and another reminds us that trial sermons are a "trial to everybody." The minister is the chief sufferer for wanting to do the best job and make sure of success with the people; by giving them his or her best sermon, the minister may let the people in for a long term of misgiving afterward if accepted as pastor. They will not have been shown a sample of his or her preaching, but the cream of it.

The story is told of one minister who was invited to preach a trial sermon in a vacant pulpit, but who refused, saying that the pulpit committee must hear him in his own church. "I am like these matches," the minister said, "that won't strike fire except on the box they come in."

In this connection, the advice of an old Methodist preacher who served many appointments is worth remembering. He said:

> When you go to a new place, never preach the best sermon you have the first time you are there. If you do, the people's expectations will be raised so high that you may never be able to satisfy them again. Don't preach your worst sermon either. Just give them a middling good stiff sermon and you have got room after that to go in either direction.

There should be no flaw in the spirit or letter of the title that gives a minister a new pulpit and parish. The question is sometimes raised as to whether a minister should accept a call on learning that it is by no means unanimous. About one-fourth of the ministers giving their opinion on this subject stated offhand that they would refuse any call unless it were unanimous. However, the majority agreed that the whole thing may depend on how large the opposing minority was and what the objections might be. If the objections are such that the minister is sure they can be overcome, given time and opportunity, well and good. One authority says that it will depend on whether the opposing minority is "reasonable or obstinate." A hostile minority of any kind is a factor to be seriously considered.

When an actual contract is to be signed between pastor and church, there usually is no difficulty, once the terms have been understood and agreed on in advance. It is unthinkable for either minister or church to break the letter or the spirit of such an agreement.

Resignation from one pulpit in order to take up work in another ought to be done in such a way as to safeguard the interests of the work one leaves. Church contracts, where there are such, usually specify that a number of months' notice shall be given by either party desiring to terminate the relationship. At any rate, a minister who decides to resign is in duty bound to do so in a formal manner and should arrange with the proper persons in regard to turning over property, records, and administrative functions.

Mutual Rights

In the relationship that exists between a pastor and the particular parish being served, both pastor and congregation should clearly understand their mutual rights under both church and civil law. Church laws differ in different places, and legal relationships and rights also vary under different charters. Often it takes a factional fight to bring out the exact legal status of mutual rights. Sometimes the minister or the church has to appeal to the state, and the arbitrary statement of a civil judge in a court of law finally outlines the rights and obligations of both parties. On such occasions, the matter may be settled according to the law, but not according to the prophets—hostility is everlastingly perpetuated. So ministerial prerogatives and oversight, trustees' control and property rights, membership rights, and the like, ought to be understood thoroughly by all parties concerned.

Anyone would be a foolish minister, of course, who constantly reminded the people that, legally, clergy have this particular right or that special privilege. Likewise, people would take the heart out of their minister by creating a feeling of suspicion concerning the pastor's control and must, therefore, set up boundaries with legal restrictions. Nevertheless the minister will do well to know the law of the church regarding the office, the law of the state of residence concerning ministerial right, and the legal points involved in any special contract with the local church—if there is a contract.

The pulpit is conceded by all as rightfully belonging to the minister. The proclamation of gospel truth is a special mission, and it is also tacitly understood that the minister must be allowed to have control of all formal worship in the church. Certain churches qualify the pastor's control of the pulpit by stipulated restrictions, but the consensus of opinion holds that the minister should have the entire control of it.

To invite into one's pulpit a minister or public speaker who is known to be unacceptable to a great portion of the congregation is of doubtful propriety. Of the ministers questioned on this matter, over half affirmed that it should never be done; the others felt that circumstances might sometimes make it permissible. When the pulpit is opened to one who represents a cause to which many persons in the church do not subscribe—for instance, certain types of political speakers or those who are pressing for some social action that will not be supported by all—the matter can become acute. The minister should remember that while the pulpit is the pastor's responsibility, there should be no fear of having the truth proclaimed from it; the people, too, have a very real equity in the church and are, after all, the ones expected to listen. In general, little good, and often much harm, is done by such procedure.

Policies against the temper of the local church should be carefully considered before the minister introduces them. The pastor may be morally right and personally strong enough to force them into effect, but the support of the people is a powerful asset. Forfeit that, and the loss is irreparable.

We have already discussed the matter of the minister's time from a professional standpoint, but this should be remembered in connection with the local church. A minister may very properly resent the implication that money can pay for services, but nevertheless there is a sense in which the pastor's time and ability do belong to the local church. No one, of course, tells the minister how to divide each day's work, but it should not be assumed that the pastor is entirely independent of the people who pay the bills.

Finances

Laypersons are expected to take over the management of church finances and, in theory at least, always do. This is well, and the ministry, with a universal sigh of relief, is glad to leave money matters entirely to the membership of the church. Some ministers take an extreme position here and even refuse to allow matters affecting the financial status of the church to be brought to their attention. This attitude on the part of a few pastors does not gain general support. The

119

majority of ministers feel that the laypeople of the church ought to be encouraged and helped by their pastor as they carry on their voluntary, and sometimes arduous, work. Certainly the minister as titular leader of the church ought at least to be sufficiently interested in the struggle the financial committee is making to set with them as counselor and to become well informed regarding the financial affairs of the parish. However, it is not felt that the minister should actually raise church money, except as the public leader in some forward-looking congregational enterprise upon which all are agreed. On the other hand, there are ministers who frankly say that they are compelled to lead their people in the matter of raising the regular budget of the church and that they have no hesitation in so doing. The tactful minister will know how to help without hindering, and how to be present without dominating the financial committee of the church.

When *church money* or any special funds are handled by the minister, accuracy is of extreme importance. Carelessness here is beyond forgiveness. More than once those who have been entrusted with funds for philanthropic or religious causes have had charges leveled against them for improper accounting, and there have been court trials and convictions in certain instances. One noted case of this sort had to do with the treasurer of a social agency whose plight was brought about, many friends firmly believed, because of poorly kept records rather than criminal intent. Whatever may have been the merits of that case, it is a fact that those who handle money—all philanthropic organizations, committees for relief, and such—should keep their books so that they may be ready for examination at a moment's notice. Let the minister watch this point carefully, for some have lost pulpits by giving adversaries an opportunity to attack them through their own carelessness.

Church Property

The minister should always remember that church property *is* the property of the church. It is very proper to consider the parsonage, or manse or rectory or whatever the house may be called, as personal property so long as the parish is being served. This should be known and appreciated by others, as trouble has sometimes been made by officious church property committees. Nevertheless the most deeply rooted pastor, geographically speaking, will do well to remember that the title to the house is held by others and that he or she is but a sojourner, as all predecessors were. This will cause reflection in the matter of taking any unusual steps with regard to church property until the responsible officials have been consulted.

Church Records

The records of the church must be kept with care, as all such records belong to the church. Protestant ministers, especially of the less centralized denominations, are woefully lacking in this. The Roman Catholic Church can teach some good lessons in preserving records of baptisms and marriages. These sometimes become extremely valuable to the persons involved, yet, few local churches make anything like farsighted preparation for keeping them. The minister must lead in this. All past records should be located and preserved, along with the current records, in an accurate and systematic way. All records and papers should be turned over to the succeeding minister with careful explanations regarding their nature.

Personal records ought to be kept by each minister and, of course, are private property. Some good system for keeping them ought to be followed. Personal records have the advantage of acting as a check on official records. The sermons a minister preaches, when and where; the marriages performed, with names, dates, and witnesses;

the baptisms (if the church practices infant baptism)—
these may be of importance in determining legal dates after
years have passed. The records would also be helpful for
persons tracing their "roots."

Publicity

The modern minister is expected to know something of
publicity methods and to use them for the benefit of the
church. Church publicity is but a phase of the great science
of advertising, which America has so well learned. Church
bulletins, illuminated signs, floodlighted churches, and
advertising stunts of all sorts are used by many ministers.
Church people take pride in frequent mention of their
church in the press and like to see the name of their
minister looming large in the church news section. This is
permissible if there is actual news value in such items.
Neighborhood newspapers are glad to get church material
when it is really news, and the minister should understand
what the local paper may consider to be of value to its
readers and should know how "news style" copy is
prepared.

It should be remembered also that the usual Monday
morning newspaper is proverbially more news hungry than
that of any other days of the week, inasmuch as Sunday
does not provide the general copy that the secular
processes of other days provide. Papers will, therefore,
quite often publish with eagerness extracts of sermons or
special events that have taken place in churches the day
before.

William H. Leach, when editor of *Church Management,*
outlined several rules for publicity, which should guide in
advertising one's church. These will be recognized as
universally valid:

1. Publicity must be *truthful.* There can be no misleading
statements, no exaggeration. As Dr. Leach says:

> It [the church] has no right to advertise a great sermon and then have the preacher enter the pulpit to utter platitudes which are already thread worn. It has no moral right to advertise a great musical service and offer a half-baked program which would be barred from any musical test.

It might be added here that even though a church may be able to deceive the people and the press on one or two occasions, this cannot be done often. Truth, like honesty, is the best policy.

2. The advertising must be *subordinate* to the thing advertised. In other words, it must be the servant, not the master, of the church. This principle will prevent an excessive expenditure for publicity and will keep all things in proportion. When publicity comes to be the chief thing about a church, when in the popular mind the name of that church is but a synonym for freak advertising stunts or a menagerie or a fashion show or talent show, then the church has gone in for a type of publicity that makes it less than a church.

3. The minister cannot afford any publicity *reflecting on his or her sincerity* or character, nor any that makes the person appear as a religious quack or freak. Someone has said that the worst comment on the American pulpit is the list of sermon topics that the usual Saturday afternoon paper carries, which exploits the morbid and the sensational. Advertising is lawful if lawfully used, but truth has a strange way of manifesting itself. The church that is fulfilling its mission soon becomes known for what it is. Lawful publicity is good, and no one pleads for the shrinking-violet church, but there is something about the blatant modern way of "telling the world" that strays from the Master's teaching. He had no condemnation for publicans and sinners equal to that which he poured out upon those who sounded a trumpet before them when they gave alms and who made long prayers in public that they might be noticed.

Publicity is a splendid thing in its place, and the modern minister should know something about it, but there is something else about which more should be known. Dr. Paul Elmer More of Princeton once lectured to a small group on Greco-Christian philosophy. "The thing the church has lost to-day," said Dr. More, "and the thing it used to have, is this"—and he went to the blackboard and wrote on it:

ταπεινοφροσύνο

In plain English, this means Christian humility or, as Archbishop Trench put it, "thinking little of one's self, because this is in a sense the right estimate for any human being no matter how great."

7

CONDUCTING PUBLIC WORSHIP

The atmosphere of public worship should be carefully guarded by the minister. Charles Jefferson says in *The Building of the Church:*

> Blessed is the preacher who converts his church into a temple, and who, with or without pictured windows and without or with the help of ritual and rich architecture, creates by the conduct of the service an atmosphere in which souls instinctively look Godward. . . . Atmosphere is everything.

This is true. The atmosphere, the overtone of the congregation gathered to worship God, is different from that found in any other place in the world. Children of the church, strangers, even scoffers, sense that atmosphere instantly. Certain ecclesiastical organizations have carefully studied this matter and make everything combine to induce a feeling of reverence and unique position—the windows, statuary, clouds of smoke from swinging censer, appealing even to the lowly sense of smell—and whatever heads may say, hearts feel that there is something transcending the ordinary in the house of God. Hymns, prayers, sermon, even announcements—all should harmonize with and add to this sense of the Presence.

The minister who does not feel this most keenly has had a faint call to what others know for a most sacred office. The person who acts as free and unrestrained in conducting public worship as if it were a golf match at the country club has not come close to the Almighty. Miserable are the people whose worship is ordered for them by such a pastor. Like priest, like people. If the minister, in the midst of a gathering of worshipers, does not feel the presence of the Most High in a unique way, how may the people feel it?

The minister in the pulpit or before the people in the church should be so aware of the sacred and peculiar place that he or she occupies that the people, too, will become aware of it and of their own place. The Urim and Thummim of the Lord should shine on the spiritual breastplate of modern ministers; when the people feel it, as though some new Sinai is smoking, they will be prepared for thunderings and lightnings and the voice of God. Let the minister before the people constantly remember these things and break not the spirit of worship, which belongs to God.

The custom of stopping the worship and asking the people in the pews to greet one another for a few moments—sometimes denominated as "The Peace"—is of doubtful propriety. It compromises both worship and the sincerity of true greeting. Both worship and enthusiastic and genuine greetings have their place among Christian people, but not mixed up together. Worship in God's house belongs to God and to him alone; no calling for an artificial human break in it ought ever to be allowed.

Conduct in the Pulpit

Nowhere more than in the pulpit should ministers display their best qualities as ladies and gentlemen. The minister is courteous not only in worship, but also in any other gathering, and what one may not say or do in the living room must certainly not be done in the house of God.

It is impossible to list all errors in pulpit decorum, but present-day ministers feel that the following are especially reprehensible:

Talking needlessly and laughing with another minister in the pulpit.

Gazing vacantly about instead of being occupied gravely and intently with the duty of the hour.

Smoothing the hair, arranging the tie, or in any way putting the finishing touch to one's personal clothing before the congregation.

Touching the face without the use of a handkerchief; blowing one's nose loudly or conspicuously.

Lounging in the chair or pulpit seat; crossing the legs "like a big four," as one man expressed it.

Failing to set an example to the people by absolute reverence in attitude and bearing when someone else is leading the prayer.

Moving needlessly about; showing anxiety over trivial details; "weaving" or rocking up and down on one's toes; putting hands in pockets; engaging in unusual mannerisms; showing a spirit of levity, absent-mindedness, slouchiness, or rudeness in any one of the innumerable ways in which these may be expressed.

There is a correct way to sit when in the pulpit—when in any public setting, for that matter. The posture should be erect but not stiff, with feet well under and in toward the chair, each resting evenly on the floor with the heel of one foot even with the instep of the other and arms close in with hands on the arms of the chair in a natural position. Such a posture gives an impression of respectful and competent alertness.

When a visiting minister or speaker is to take part in a regular service, it is customary for the minister in charge to introduce him or her to the congregation. A simple, yet gracious, introduction is in much better taste than an effusive one. It is well to be explicit as to the initials and title of the visitor and to pronounce the name correctly. If there is a noteworthy fact that should be given to the congregation, this may be stated briefly. Anything, however, hinting of eulogy or extravagant commendation is always best avoided in introductions, in church and out. Let the speaker's own merits stand with the message delivered.

When a speaker concludes an address or sermon, it is always in good taste for the presiding minister to assume charge again quietly to give the order for the next part of the program. Comment by the presiding minister is risky and difficult. He or she cannot hope to speak at the point where the other speaker concluded and may mar the spirit under which the audience has been left, if an attempt is made to comment on the message. The minister should show by actions rather than words his or her own feeling and, by quietly giving out the number of the concluding hymn, for instance, may add to and not break the spirit of the message. If the message has been a good one, the people know it and need not be told; if it was poor, they know that too, and the person who attempts to make them believe otherwise has a huge task. It is better, therefore, to refrain from comment after a speech or sermon, though this rule, like any other, may be broken when occasion demands.

Preparation

The minister feels it a professional duty, as well as an ethical and religious one, to be prepared beforehand for the conduct of every service. Circumstances, of course, occasionally force the minister into situations where it is impossible to make preparation worthy of the name, but the service is always the poorer when this happens. Ministers of all denominations condemn a colleague who comes unprepared when assuming leadership of public worship.

This matter of preparation is commonly taken to refer to preparation for preaching, but all churches, even the strictly nonliturgical, are coming to place more and more emphasis on the various parts of the service other than the preaching. No longer are we thinking in terms of preaching alone, but, as Dr. Jefferson has put it, the whole service from the first note of the prelude to the last note of the organ is worship. So preparation on the minister's part has to do with many things. Does he or she feel personally prepared? What is the scripture lesson, and will it be read as it should be read? Is the minister ready to lead the prayers? Fortunately, most parts of the church service, like the vital functions of life, become matters of routine—that is to say, habit. Where there is to be no special variation of the regular order of worship, the minister is left free to prepare for the sermon and other parts that must necessarily be different in each recurrent service and need not be concerned about the invariable parts of the order of worship, which come to be as familiar as the fit of one's own clothes.

When a special service is to take place or a special feature to be introduced, all should be carefully arranged beforehand. Suppose another minister is to preach. Details regarding the essential parts of the service should be explained in advance. The necessary consultation between ministers should take place before the service and not before the people. Anything that savors of lack of preparation—apparent attempts to select hymns or to settle on a passage of scripture to be read—mars the atmosphere of worship.

Preparation for a minister's own part in the worship is not merely a matter of intellectual application, or "cramming," on a sermon outline at the last minute, but rests on a personal spiritual need or desire. The quiet hour before the service, the prayer in private, the cultivation of the Presence—these sometimes mean more than subhead *b* in division 3 of the sermon. The ancient church stressed this matter officially, and one of the finest and best-loved prayers of the Middle Ages was given to the priest to say for himself in private before he went out to the people to celebrate the Sacrament:

> Almighty God, unto whom all hearts are open, all desires known, and from whom no secrets are hid; cleanse the thoughts of our hearts by the inspiration of thy Holy Spirit, that we may perfectly love thee, and worthily magnify thy Holy Name; through Christ our Lord.

Nonliturgical churches, while they have never prescribed any system for private preparation, have always insisted on the thing itself—none more so than the fathers of the great evangelical communions.

Many ministers have a *prayer with the members of the choir* just before a service begins. This has the double advantage of giving the minister a chance to act as pastor for the members of the choir and of impressing upon them the joint responsibility they share with the minister as leaders in Christian worship.

Order of Worship

Liturgical churches have usually prescribed a formal *processional,* and in this their respective customs and uses are authoritative. Nonliturgical churches also have increasingly adopted the processional, and here the custom of each individual church will be determinative.

Where there is a formal processional, especially in the larger churches, timeless protocol seems to call for the ranking minister or ministers to be last in the procession. This is a procedure observed among other organized bodies, especially schools of higher education. Presidents and deans follow last in their formal processional ceremonies, as do bishops in episcopally organized denominations, when bishops are present. Also, strict liturgists insist that such ranking persons should see that a perceptible space be kept between themselves and the preceding group (such as a choir) as they march in. But such minor matters, and even processionals themselves, are not considered of great importance and, of course, in small congregations are usually disposed of entirely.

In churches where there is no processional, or where the minister takes his or her place within the chancel independently of the choir's entrance, good use prescribes that the pastor be somewhat secluded from the people until the time for the service. There is nothing binding about this, and, in small churches where there is no private room for the minister, it is not out of place to wait quietly with the people before "church begins." However, where there is a study or office in the church, usually the minister finds it more convenient to remain there in meditation and private prayer before leading the service.

In those churches that do not conform to an ordered processional, the actual entrance of the minister should be dignified, but not ostentatious. Henry Ward Beecher said that he abhorred "the formal, stately and solemn entrance of the man whose whole appearance seems to call upon all to see how holy he is." There should be the quiet, natural assurance of one who knows that he or she is going into the pulpit to lead the people Godward.

Punctuality is a necessity in beginning a service. Let the

minister appear before the congregation at the announced time of the service, or a moment or two beforehand, perhaps during the organ prelude, if there is one. In modern churches, the pastor's study quite often opens on the pulpit. Where there is a visiting minister or ministers the pastor acts as usher for them, leading the way until the pulpit platform is reached, then stepping aside to indicate what seats the guests are to occupy. The central seat, if there is more than one, is generally assigned to the preacher of the hour or to the guest of honor. Sometimes, however, it is preferred that the local minister keep the central seat as presiding officer.

It has been traditional for ministers in evangelical denominations to bow or kneel for a private prayer after they have entered the chancel or pulpit. Present-day ministers are somewhat divided regarding the propriety of this, many feeling that such a prayer smacks of ostentation. However, others take the position that a minister's sincerity must be taken for granted unless there is proof to the contrary. A prominent minister observed that one cannot expect the people to be in a worshipful attitude if the minister is not. It is generally agreed that the custom of each individual church in this regard should be followed.

The actual service in many churches begins with a formal *call to worship,* which may be said or sung according to the practice of the respective churches. Where the minister gives the call, it should be remembered that the tone of voice, as well as its strength and inflection, has a bearing on the atmosphere that is to prevail. A certain reverent strength in summons or proclamation is needed, but stridency or explosiveness must be avoided. It is "the silver trumpet," not a brass one, that calls "to holy convocations," according to Christopher Wordsworth's great hymn.

It is the custom in many churches for *hymns* to be

announced on a bulletin board or perhaps by means of a printed bulletin; sometimes scripture readings are also thus announced. The service then proceeds without oral announcement. This is an agreeable practice where the people have been accustomed to it and makes for a smoothly running service. It has the disadvantage of suggesting a certain leaderless impersonality in the worship. Announcement of the hymns by the minister is an opportunity to "float" the service along and to comment occasionally on the words or music of the hymn to be sung. People respond to helpful public leadership.

When the minister is to give out the number of the hymn, let it be done authoritatively and in such a way that all may hear. It may be necessary to repeat the number, as there are persons in every congregation who, having ears, hear not, even when they are listening. Hymns "listlessly announced" were deprecated by John Barbour when lecturing on "Ministers and Music." He insisted that the "pastor is the leader of the praise. . . . The people will always take their key and cue from him. If he slight, hurry over or make nothing of the praise services, the majority of the people will treat them the same way."

An experienced leader of public worship will occasionally give out the number of the hymn, then read the first line of it or call its name, then give out the number again. This is often a good plan. As a rule, the minister should let the organ and choir take the hymn as it is written and sing it through. However, for the sake of lightening a service, some ministers adopt the plan of calling for the repetition of certain stanzas or they exhort the people to sing with more spirit or call attention, as John Wesley urged should be done, to the words being sung. People like to sing, and the wise minister, lets them sing on. Choirs and church music are traditionally uncertain factors, and when they are working well, let them work.

When the people are singing, let the minister also stand and sing. In *The Art of Preaching,* Charles R. Brown has this to say to the minister:

> Sing yourself! Do it as a means of grace to your own soul! Do it also as a bit of godly example to your people. The lazy, shiftless minister who announces a hymn and then goes back to his chair and sits down while the people stand up and sing it, as if praising God were no affair of his, ought to be cast out of the synagogue. Unless he is a semi-invalid almost too weak to be there at all, he ought to be pitched out of his pulpit forthwith by some athletic deacon ordained of God as the Scripture says, "to purchase to himself a good degree and great boldness in the faith" by thus exercising his authority as an officer of the church militant.

Needless to say, hymns should be carefully chosen with a clear understanding of what the people know as well as what may be appropriate for the occasion or topic. Sometimes, a hymn that is suitable in language and theme may prove difficult in music, and occasionally a hymn chosen because the first line seems to emphasize a certain theme has many other lines that decidedly deal with other matters. The minister should remember this when looking for "something appropriate" to go with the message. Fortunately for worship, every good hymn has a unity of its own, which transcends and sometimes defies hymnal indexing. A familiar hymn, well sung, is appropriate almost anywhere.

In general, the first hymn should be one that is well known by all in order to draw the congregation together immediately in a unity of praise and thanksgiving. New hymns are indeed to be taught the people, and each pastor should have a plan for doing so—but not at the beginning of regular worship. A point later in the service may provide an opportunity to learn a less familiar hymn, or one may be carefully chosen to fit in with the sermon or special theme of the day. It is not a good plan to choose too somnolent a hymn or too lulling a tune just before the sermon. If the people are to be put to sleep, don't let the singing do it!

The final hymn may aptly sum up or close the service with a note of aspiration, challenge, or conquest, or it may be one of the robust marching songs of the church. A recessional, of course, does something of this in its own way.

Practices differ considerably in the matter of public prayer. The liturgical churches provide fixed and majestic forms of prayer to direct both minister and people in divine praise. In the nonliturgical churches, however, and in all congregations in which extemporaneous prayer is used, certain general observations on this important matter may be made:

Prayer is addressed to God, not the people. If this is understood, it will keep all prayer reverent, humble, and quiet. John A. Broadus, in his book *Preparation and Delivery of Sermons,* said that in public prayer the minister should "earnestly endeavor to realize what he is doing." He is talking to God. We have all heard prayers that stormed the skies, when the voice and tones of the suppliant made the rafters ring. If this is natural to the person, then it must be respected, but most ministers feel that God will not hear us for our loud speaking any more than for our lengthy speaking, nor do we ordinarily think of him as off on a long journey or, perhaps, asleep. We instinctively feel that reverence is shown by quiet. Dr. Broadus illustrated this by quoting a statement by R. L. Dabney, from his *Sacred Rhetoric:*

> The *utterance* of prayer "should be softer, more level,...less vehement, more subdued. Every tone should breathe tenderness and supplication. . . . It is dificult to say which is more unsuitable to this sacred exercise—a hurried, perfunctory utterance, as of one who reads some tiresome or trivial matter, a violent and declamatory manner, as though one had ventured upon objurgation of his Maker, or a headlong and confused enunciation."

135

Since prayer is addressed to God, it is incorrect for the one praying to speak of God as a third person. This is sometimes done, and there are a few ministers who state that they do not consider it wrong; however, the overwhelming number hold that it is. Certainly it seems incongruous both logically and devotionally to refer to God in a prayer to God.

Quite a noteworthy change has come about within recent years in the way God is addressed in prayer. The traditional *thee* and *thou,* which have been invariably used since the first prayer book in English in 1549, have been supplanted in favor of the familiar *you* of ordinary speech. This change came rather swiftly into general use. The substitution of *you* for thee in prayer began with pious laymen in their public prayer as they spoke what came naturally to them, since Elizabethan English had long been superseded.

This "modernization" of pronouns referring to the deity has been to the extreme distaste of many, especially older persons who have been brought up with familiarity to the older forms. Those who do continue to use the old formal language of prayer should be careful about their verb endings when the second personal pronoun is being used. It is "thou" who "hast," not who "hath"; who "lovest," not "loveth," and so on. Reading the well-furnished liturgies of the past will help a minister in this respect as in many other ways.

Since in prayer the minister addresses God, he or she should not at the same time attempt to address the audience or put out ideas for purely human consumption. "To pray for another minister present with elaborate compliment, is a sadly frequent, and grossly improper practice," Dr. Broadus affirmed. Anything in prayer that hints of making a speech to the audience or of giving information for the benefit of the congregation is bad. No true prayer can be filled with didactic affirmations and thou-knowest-this and thou-knowest-that tidbits of human news gathering. Prayer is unto God.

Dean W. L. Sperry, writing in *Religion and Life,* held that the great fault of extemporaneous prayer is didacticism, or giving information for the benefit of the congregation rather than God. As he put it:

> The informational serpent in the grass . . . is forever creeping into extempore prayer. We are all aware of this liability . . . yet how hard it is to keep clear in pastoral prayer of that mental process by which we give information either to God or to the congregation. Once we start with the preface, "O God, thou knowest . . . " or "O God, we are gathered here together, and thou seest . . . " the serpent has raised its head in our Eden.

The minister prays for—that is, in behalf of and in place of—the entire congregation. This should keep him or her from expressing personal private feelings or emotions too decidedly. Since the minister is the mouthpiece of all, any tendency toward giving way to expressing personal sentiments or opinions should be carefully watched. In this regard, thought and study beforehand will help the minister lead the people. Some of the most prominent preachers in the country declare that they put almost as much time on studying their formal pastoral prayer for each Sunday as they do on the sermon they are to preach. Presbyterian ministers have traditionally set the rest of the clergy a good example here.

Pulpit prayers can become "grooved" before the pray-er knows it, and many a nonliturgical minister who refuses to be guided by a "book of prayer forms" unconsciously drops into a prayer pattern that is as fixed as anything in the Prayer Book and far inferior in language and thought.

Prayers should not be long. If anyone wishes to disagree with this statement, it may be amended to "prayers should not be *too* long." Asked about the length of their pulpit prayers, present-day ministers show quite a difference of opinion. The average length is between three and five minutes, with some making it "four to six," some "five or seven," and one or two suggesting "anywhere up to ten minutes." But the long pastoral prayer of earlier days has definitely been much shortened. George Whitefield once rebuked a man who prayed a long prayer by saying: "Sir, you prayed me into a good frame, and then you prayed me out of it."

Prayer is not expected to take the place of the sermon in formal worship. Dr. Nathaniel J. Burton tells of a minister who told the Lord so much in an opening prayer that the speaker of the occasion had no thunder, and not much heart, left. Prayer has a field all its own in both public and private worship. Happy is the minister who can commune with God in the presence of the congregation.

The correct posture in prayer has always been a debatable matter, and the custom of each individual's church is to be respected in each instance. Prayer ought, of course, to be audible to all, and as Dr. Broadus warned, hands are not to be placed before one's face nor should the head be so bent down as to stifle utterance. "We must also avoid contortions of countenance, and tricks of posture and gesture, which there will always be some persons to notice."

With the use of the pulpit microphone and amplifier systems, a matter of practical technique is called for on the part of the minister. When the microphone is firmly fixed on the pulpit, the minister, both in prayer and preaching, finds it necessary to speak directly into it. No natural moving about can be allowed, for the old "square of the distance" comes into play, and the slightest moving closer or moving further from the microphone will amplify or diminish the sound of the voice doubly more than might be expected. The same "range" at all times is carefully to be kept to secure effective delivery.

With a fixed pulpit microphone, the minister cannot kneel for public prayer, though where kneeling is definitely called for, as at the communion table in Episcopal and United Methodist churches, a separate microphone can be arranged in needed places. Prominent speakers, actors, and many ministers prefer, when possible, to have a microphone attached to their bodies, as this will allow a natural moving about in their speaking. Such a mike will obviate the variations that, as mentioned above, may occur with a fixed microphone and will provide the best method of electric vocal magnification.

Scripture readings should be selected and studied beforehand. Public reading of the scriptures is not always easy, and to do it well, familiarity with the thought as well as the words is essential. It is, however, a richly rewarding part of the service, and people long to hear the Bible read so that it may speak its own message to them. Good authorities suggest that pronunciation should be carefully studied, and where "indelicate expressions as we see it" occur, these may be omitted or expressed according to some different version.

Commenting on the scripture lesson while reading it does not please the majority of ministers polled. "Give it to the people unvarnished," they say. "Let the Word be its own witness." But quite a number take the other position and say that it is perfectly all right for ministers to comment as they read if they feel so inclined—they are "expounders of the Word of God." All agree that ambiguous or difficult turns of expression may profitably be explained when a word or two will suffice, and many ministers who say that they never comment on the scripture while reading it advise taking time to "give the setting of the lesson" before they actually begin to read.

As a rule, obscure scripture lessons are to be avoided. All scripture should be read slowly and impressively so that the teenagers in the last pew will be able to understand.

Responsive reading calls for a technique all its own. The minister "sets the pace" and the tone by reading the first line, couplet, or verse. The leader may err either by going too fast or by picking up the first word of the next sentence before the people have completed the last of theirs. This jumping ahead on the part of the minister communicates a certain jittery feeling to the respondents and makes for uneasiness. A good leader will know how to set a verbal pace that will be strong and sure, yet not too slow, and will thus guide the people to do their part more evenly. A great many ministers open the pulpit Bible reverently when they first come into the pulpit and close it reverently as the service ends. But there are others who state that they wait until the actual time to read the lesson before they open the Bible and that they close it when the lesson ends. Others say that they keep the Bible open at all times, that it is never closed; while still others see that the Bible is open as the service begins, and they let someone else close it after all worshipers have gone.

Protestant churches find something symbolic in the open Bible. It is the charter and warrant for all that the Church stands for. While a crass bibliolatry is not to be implied, all agree that casual or thoughtless treatment of the Bible, such as slamming it about or banging on it, is forbidden by reverent good taste.

The giving of announcements is part of the service in practically all churches today, although a printed bulletin often provides an ideal medium through which this may be done. Announcements in church are not new in the history of public worship; the Church of England in the first Prayer Book of Edward VI four hundred years ago had a rubric calling for the priest to announce what holy days were to be kept, what marriage banns were to be published, and so on. It is not, therefore, to be considered a "break" in ordered worship when the modern minister takes time to announce some special event or to emphasize some particular duty. However, announcements that are trivial and trite will sometimes seem to interrupt the even flow of a service of worship; and where a printed bulletin is provided to take care of such matters it should be depended on to do so. Otherwise, let the minister make all announcements worthy of public notice in a dignified way at the very beginning of the worship service.

In some churches, it is the custom for a lay officer to make the announcements on the principle that temporal affairs and the mechanics of church life are properly under the management of the laity. Announcements, if made at all, should be made well. When announcements are printed in a bulletin, any public reading of them is a waste of needed time. However, while ministers all agree that this is a good rule, many admit that they break it from time to time when some particular matter needs to be especially emphasized.

Since there is a stated time for announcements, they should be made at that time and not interspersed throughout other parts of the service. It is not wise to emphasize an announcement or to repeat one just before the benediction. While the people's heads are bowed in quiet for the final blessing, such an announcement breaks into the peace in which they should be allowed to depart.

Taking an offering in church is another custom of great antiquity and has long been firmly entrenched as a part of the service among American Protestant chuches. Some churches dislike the public passing of the plate and prefer other means of securing funds. Private subscriptions, or even a box for contributions at the door of the church, are sometimes substituted. But the time-honored passing of the plate is not likely soon to disappear, and the people, as they give their gifts, have an opportunity to participate directly in the service.

When a public collection is taken, it should be done quietly and efficiently. The laypersons of the church usually have this matter in hand, and it seems more in keeping with the spirit of the offering for one of the laypersons to supervise it and stand as a representative of the church while it is being taken. However, in certain of the liturgical churches the minister manages these matters, and the presentation of the offering is a formal ministerial act. As different churches have different methods and ceremonies connected with the taking and receiving of the offering, no more need be said on this. It should be remembered, however, that the offering is and should be a true part of the people's worship and when carried out in that spirit becomes a blessing to the givers.

Some have felt that the minister should put his or her contribution in the plate like any other person in the congregation. This is rarely done and would be difficult to arrange without causing the minister to appear either awkward or ostentatious.

Every minister should, of course, give what's possible to the church budget and see that the contribution reaches the church treasurer regularly. This should be done out of his or her own salary and as a personal contribution, not as something previously "allowed" out of a hypothetically larger salary. Ministers have sometimes been criticized for their failure to see that their own personal financial contribution is at least as large as that of any other person of equivalent salary in the congregation.

The Sermon

There are many able and comprehensive books about preaching; both the preparation and the delivery of sermons have been treated exhaustively by competent authorities. Certain major principles are involved, and the minister would do well to heed a word or two of general caution.

When a minister preaches, let it be *natural*. This is the injunction of all experienced ministers as they speak to their younger colleagues. There must be no imitation of another, no cant, no "holy whine." If God has truly called a minister, he or she will have a message to be delivered through his or her own personality.

Chief faults in sermon delivery, as listed by prominent ministers, are: using a "holy tone" or any unnatural voice; "oh-ing" and "ah-ing"; poor enunciation; studied oratory for dramatic effect; yelling and pulpit pounding; inaudibility; following notes or manuscript too closely; singsong delivery; explosiveness; rising on toes; walking about too much; shifting from one leg to the other; acrobatics; facial contortions, looking at the ceiling or the floor instead of people; preaching to the front half of the congregation, or to those on one side, rather than to all; using hands too much; holding gown with both hands or putting hands in pockets when preaching; preaching not for a verdict but for approval or to get through; prolonging the conclusion.

There are, of course, many other faults that might be listed, and personal mannerisms are almost as numerous as persons. Of mannerisms, however, it may be said that some of these may actually enhance the attractiveness of a popular speaker or beloved pastor, as they seem to belong to the essence of the person.

Someone once asked Henry Ward Beecher what he thought of sensational preaching. He answered that he was against it, if by *it* was meant a low temporary success by mere trickery, but if *it* meant "preaching that produced a sensation" he was for it. His meaning is clear: The gospel itself is revolutionary. There is enough truth in the gospel to provide all the sensation any minister may consistently inaugurate and sustain, but claptrap methods and gaudy attempts to "catch the crowd" have but one end—they run out, and their promoter usually is compelled to run out with them.

Personal mention in sermons should be carefully handled. There is an instinctive reverence for the preaching of the Word, which the ages have taught people to feel, and it is not always wise to encroach upon that reverence by pulling in little details of local interest or adding personal allusions that are commonplace in the minds of the people. On the other hand, sometimes these local references are easily understood and serve to fasten the thought of the sermon in the minds of the hearers. It is a matter on which every minister must judge with an individual evaluation each time. Jesus certainly dealt with everyday life. Personal allusions, however, or narrative adventures and opinions of the speaker must be watched, lest the appearance of egotism be given. Ministers everywhere agree that personal references are to be used very sparingly, if at all.

The calling of personal names, references to persons in the audience by name, and such, is not considered in good taste. In fact, in legislative bodies and all formal public assemblies, the use of names is avoided. It is "Mr. Chairman" or "the gentleman from Mississippi" or "the chairman of the committee," not "Dr. Jones" or "Senator Smith." The same atmosphere of formality holds in public worship, and the "reading out in meeting" of private names is to be avoided wherever possible.

The use of slang ought also to be watched. Slang, since it is a linguistic outlaw, is all the more powerful, and many a minister sometimes resorts to it to drive home a point in an unforgettable way. Yet its use should be guarded, for if it becomes habitual, its power will be weakened and the aversion felt toward it by the "purists" in the audience will overbalance its value as an effective instrument.

Scolding people, especially those present in lieu of those absent, is in bad taste as well as bad temper. In fact, no minister or public speaker should ever admit to being piqued at the size of the audience, and as a rule one does better to make no comment at all about the number present. If the congregation is large, one may act as though large congregations are, of course, expected; if the audience is disappointingly small, the minister flatters those present by giving them the best performance possible and acting as though they are equal to a great multitude.

A minister should not correct disorder in such a way as to bring about greater disorder. It should, however, be said that a minister will do well to see that the service of worship is treated with respect by all present. If disturbing noises outside the building can be eliminated by a request from a layperson of the church or by some other authority, the minister is right in demanding that the people suffer no interruption from that source. Likewise, when interruptions or disorder occur in the audience during the service or during the sermon, the minister serves both the people and the message by seeing to it that this does not continue. The best plan is for the minister simply to stop preaching or to stop the service until perfect quiet reigns, then to go on. A pause of half a minute is usually sufficient. No comment need be made; just wait for quiet. It will not be long before the persons responsible will take the hint and either sit in quiet or cease to appear in that particular church. Fortunately, it appears that disorderly conduct in church—talking, laughing, and so on—has pretty well disappeared with the cruder manners of an earlier pioneer day.

Taking someone else's message and giving it as one's own is known as *plagiarism.* It is condemned by all ministers and defined differently by all. However, the honest minister will know when he or she takes what is in reality the work of another. All ministerial codes and ministers everywhere condemn plagiarism, though they recognize that everyone is indebted to those who have spoken or written before them and that often the thoughts and minds of the great leaders of the Christian pulpit must, perforce, be followed. But indebtedness for general thinking or even for a special approach is one thing, and taking the direct words or the individual sermonic creation of another is something else. No exact rule can be given

145

that will truly and exactly define plagiarism, but when a minister feels compelled to take the message or words of another, due credit should be carefully given or, at any rate, the minister must indicate that his or her thinking has at this point been directly influenced.

Conclusion of the Service

A formal *ascription* closes the sermon in certain liturgical churches, and in the nonliturgical there is often an extemporaneous prayer. This should be brief and devotional and, of course, in line with the general theme of the discourse.

It has long been the custom to "let the people go" with a benediction that will complete the service and perpetuate as much as possible the atmosphere of worship. Whether this benediction is given from the pulpit or elsewhere, as at the conclusion of the recessional, will depend on the pattern of worship followed by the respective churches.

In many churches, an opportunity for momentary silence or meditation is provided after the benediction. During this meditation, the people, of course, remain in their places. The organist may softly play a few bars during this meditative period, and after that the entire service is over. The choir or organist in many churches often sings or plays a musical amen.

Some ministers encourage their people to leave the sanctuary immediately and quietly after the worship service has concluded. Others feel that the easy exchanges of greeting among the people and the talk of friends as they prepare to leave are a part of the "communion of the saints" and not to be frowned on. Christian fellowship is certainly the tie that binds.

It is a widespread custom among churches for the minister to stand at the door of the church and greet the people as they leave. A few have felt that greeting the people at the door seems to imply the desire on the minister's part to be complimented on the sermon. However, the vast majority of pastors are thinking far more of their church and their people than of themselves at this time, and they realize the opportunity they have of doing an amazing amount of pastoral work as their people pass by them. A handshake, a word of inquiry about an absent loved one, a comment on some matter of personal interest, a welcome to a visitor—all such reap a rich pastoral reward. Some ministers, of course, have more ability at this sort of thing than others, but a warmhearted "doorway pastorate" can be most effective.

8

FUNERALS

A minister in charge of a funeral is often in one of the most difficult of situations. The pastor represents God, under whose watch-care all events, even death, take place. The minister represents humanity in its efforts to ease the bitterness of the hour, and at the same time represents an ecclesiastical organization and profession in conducting a public service. The keynote of correct conduct in all these various relationships will be found in quietness and a calm, assured attitude in both voice and bearing. Anything that breaks into the calm surety of the atmosphere will be a hindrance to the proper conduct of this service. This is the general guiding principle. Loud or strident tones, harsh singing, or even expressions that break in upon the peace of death should be carefully guarded against.

Church Funeral

If the funeral is held in a church, quite often there is a *processional*. The officiating minister usually meets the

149

body at the church door as the pallbearers bring it up the steps. The pastor's conduct should be quiet and reverent. There should be no unnecessary talking or movement on the part of anyone.

It is the custom of some ministers to go first to the home of the deceased and accompany the funeral procession to the church. This gives an opportunity for a private prayer with the family before the formalities of the actual funeral begin. But the great majority of ministers reporting on this matter follow the time-honored English custom of "meeting the corpse at the church door and proceeding before it"—that is, into the church.

The first prayer book that seems to have influenced the funeral rite in most Protestant churches, directed:

> The Priest and Clerkes meeting the Corps at ye entrance of the Church-yard and going before it either into the Church or towardes the grave, shall say or sing: *I am the resurrection and the life* (sayth the Lord . . . etc.)

This established the order for the minister or ministers to precede immediately the body when that is borne down the aisle, while reading such words as the church may provide for the occasion, or as the minister selects.

When processional sentences are read, this should be done in a distinct, but not overly loud, tone with care to see that the organist does not play even a subdued tune at that time. Actual chanting of the processional sentences on the part of the minister, as was sometimes heard in an earlier day, is not at all found among present-day Protestant ministers; in fact, many omit reading processional sentences at all. When they are used, the reading should cease about the time the body is placed before the altar or pulpit or "chancel rail." When several ministers are present, they march two by two in the procession; the one who reads the sentences goes in front of all.

Where there is no formal processional, the minister

either accompanies the family to the church and then makes his or her way unostentatiously into the pulpit or chancel, or waits at the church and goes into the pulpit slightly before the service is to begin. The minister then commences the service with readings or prayers, or perhaps there is music. In some instances, the minister walks in the processional but does not read any processional sentences. Certain ministers and denominations look with less favor on the reading of processional sentences than on the actual processional itself.

As to readings and prayers, the occasion calls, not for trumpet blasts, but for the quiet and soothing pronouncement of the magnificent words that from time immemorial have been the consolation of the bereaved. As different churches have different selections, no more need be said at this point.

When extemporaneous prayer forms part of the funeral service, the minister will wish to be more careful in this than in any other formal prayer. The pastor must not wound the feelings and susceptibilities of the grief-stricken, nor must one do violence to one's own conceptions of the providence of God. Usually even the nonliturgical ministers gradually evolve in their recurrent ministration of their own "funeral prayer," and this, with minor variations, they repeat at each funeral. A truly sympathetic pastor will have no trouble in suiting the prayer to each occasion of this sort. The funeral prayer should not be too long.

Concerning singing at funerals, the hymns that are used must, of course, be in keeping with the occasion. A few well-trained voices are much better—a quartet, for instance—than a large number of singers. The whole program for a formal funeral should be worked out carefully beforehand, and a number of copies of the program may well be made out and given to those who are to take part. Then when a hymn is to be sung, the minister

151

in charge, with a nod to the choir, may so indicate. Likewise, other ministers who have been asked to take part will more easily fulfill their duty at the designated time without need of spoken announcement. This makes for a more orderly and reverent service than would harsh announcements.

The practice of preaching a formal funeral sermon is now generally discontinued. It came to full strength over a hundred years ago in the evangelical churches of the United States, but as it led to numerous abuses and absurdities, the traditional "funeral sermon" has now almost disappeared except in certain localities. However, about half the ministers reporting their practice in this regard state that they make "brief remarks" or usually have some sort of short homily or message of comfort as a part of their service. Others state flatly that they simply read the funeral service and let the majestic words of scripture and of Christian hope be the message.

In the traditional funeral sermon of the past, ministers were commonly expected to eulogize the character of the departed, and so ran the risk, as John A. Broadus said, of giving "the lie to all their ordinary preaching." Every minister, of course, wishes to comfort the bereaved and to say what good one can of each person whose life's record is about to be closed, but honesty and candor must not be forfeited in the process. The impersonal phrases of the burial service are certainly much better than the attempt to steer between the Scylla of family grief and the Charybdis of the majesty of the judgment of God. Watching this dangerous feat of navigation and inwardly commenting on it are always to be found many persons who knew the late lamented far better than the officiating minister. Let the pastor, therefore, either stick to the written form or make remarks of a general nature, which stress the timeless verities of the gospel. It must also be remembered that other funerals are yet to be held, and the minister who goes "all out" for one person's father or husband or son or daughter will have other sons or wives or fathers or mothers in days to come. If the pastor has been extravagant in remarks about the excellencies of one of the members, it will be expected for the others as well. It is for these reasons that experienced ministers state that they use a printed service and avoid all personal remarks if possible.

It must be admitted, however, that where a pastor in a few words can tactfully say something that will serve to individualize the particular person whose funeral is being conducted, the brief sentences will be remembered and appreciated by the family and friends more than all the rest of the service. Some ministers make a point of securing from the family a few facts about the life of the deceased—birth, family record, date of death. This was the way Washington Gladden advised doing it, weaving these annals into a brief message of hope and faith. Broadus said that when references are made to a person at a funeral, they must be "scrupulously true, though not necessarily *all* the truth, for this would often be superfluous and sometimes painful." He advised that when the departed was a Christian that fact should be stressed.

The funeral rite in church is generally closed by the statement, "The service will be continued at the cemetery," or, in the case of a private interment, a mention of that fact. The ministers then leave the pulpit and precede the coffin up the aisle in a slow procession. The people should quietly stand and wait until the family, following the pallbearers, have left the church. In the meanwhile, the ministers have preceded the body to the hearse, where they stand while the coffin is being put in place. When the doors of the hearse are closed on the coffin, ministers may then seek the places provided for them in the funeral procession.

Tradition prescribes a certain order in the position of the clergy, funeral director, pallbearers, hearse, and family in a funeral procession. The funeral director, as the one in charge of such matters, indicates to each participant what place he or she is to assume in the march. Usually the funeral director leads the procession in order to clear the way and to indicate the route to be followed. The clergy come next, preceding all but the funeral director.

When the funeral party arrives at the cemetery, the minister should go at once to the hearse, standing as a sort of guard while the flowers are being taken to the grave and other preparations are made. When the procession starts, the pastor precedes the body to the grave while the coffin is "made ready to be lowered."

The prayers and readings given in the open air may be spoken in a stronger way than within a building, but the tone of quiet firmness should not be dropped.

The committal, which is the heart of the final service, was formerly objected to by many as savoring of a priestly commendation. The Presbyterians for a long time would have nothing resembling it; John Wesley, when he gave a prayer book to American Methodism in 1784, deleted the committal from his office for the burial of the dead. Methodism, however, in the middle of the nineteenth century replaced the committal in the burial service, and many manuals in use among Presbyterian preachers call for this ceremony if desired. Dr. Gladden expressed a well-balanced Protestant view when he said that the English committal service is almost identical to that employed in German Lutheran churches and "is always appropriate." There seems to be no special objection to it today in Protestantism. The wording, even in the Prayer Book, has been so altered that no warrant may be found for the statement that commendation implies any more than does the whole ceremony of Christian burial.

Present-day ministers are almost unanimous, however, in feeling that the committal should be said by the pastor of the deceased, if present, and the service is usually so arranged. The first part of the outdoor service—known in the English Prayer Book as "Anthems at the Grave"—may be assigned to an assisting minister, and so may the benediction, but ministers all agree that the committal itself belongs to the pastor or ranking minister.

A majority of the ministers approached on this subject indicate that they object to the "ashes to ashes, dust to dust" phrases of the traditional committal. The ground of their objection, as expressed by one minister, is that the previous service has been one of hope, but now "as clods are thrown upon the coffin the ominous words 'earth to earth' bring our heavenly thoughts down with a shudder and we go away with a heavy sense of having left our loved ones in the cold ground." The spirit of the objection may be understood, and every minister must do what seems best. Tougher minded clergy see nothing to object to in this regard, since the traditional committal does not so much emphasize the "dust to dust" expression as it does the majestic expectation of Christian consummation and hope. There are various forms of this committal prayer, and ministers of nonliturgical churches can easily evolve or find for themselves a prayer suitable to them.

The coffin should be lowered to the bottom of the grave for committal.

Home Funeral

The funeral service at the house of the deceased may be conducted along the same lines as described above, but is somewhat less formal. The same hints, however, as to a program prepared in advance may well be taken. While the funeral director is in actual charge of all arrangements, it is the minister who is popularly thought of as being in control. The pastor should act accordingly. It does no good to stand about the home for a considerable time before the service begins.

Often when the minister arrives, the members of the family ask to see him or her. In most cases, the minister finds that some special request or some final wishes are then made known. Occasionally, the pastor is called upon to speak to the sorrowing for the purpose of consolation. Here the quiet assurance of an intimate prayer with the members of the family can often be of inestimable help. Great tact, however, and something like canny wisdom are often called for on the part of the minister. Before the service, the people of the house are keyed up for the ordeal; guests are present, and sometimes there are curious onlookers. This may force artificiality on the part of the home people. In a few instances, there will be relatives whose grief is partially assumed. They feel that everyone expects them to show how much they cared for the loved one by "carrying on"—and carry on they will. Ministers occasionally stumble into a situation of this sort. In such cases, it sometimes happens that people who enjoy loosing the emotions really work themselves up into hysterics, or faints, and the minister is called to labor with such persons. The minister is there to induce a calmer, saner, more Christian way of facing death. Of course, sometimes a genuine and deep grief calls for and exhorts expression. It is then that only God can help, and the minister must lean on the Lord's grace in these moments.

At a Funeral Home

What has been said regarding the church funeral and the home funeral is applicable to the service conducted in a funeral chapel, or "funeral home." Somewhat less formal than a church, somewhat more so than a private residence, these institutions have come to be a feature of modern life. Naturally the funeral director prefers that each funeral he or she is called upon to manage shall be held in the establishment that has been arranged and appointed for special purpose. The clergy and the churches have been the more ready to acquiesce in the use of funeral homes since the heating of the church building in winter, the summoning of the janitor, arranging for the organist, and so on require administrative time, effort, and expense. And as a private residence is not usually large enough or suitably appointed for a public ceremony, the funeral home has, understandably enough, come to supplant both church and residence. However, there is a move to conduct more funerals from the church as the most fitting place for the funeral service.

There is, of course, no processional in a funeral home, for the body is usually resting in state there. The minister takes his or her place at the pulpit or lectern and begins with readings and prayers. The service is somewhat more brief than that at a church, though the minister should remember that each funeral is the *only* funeral to the particular people who feel its dread presence.

There is quite often a brief processional out of the funeral home, with the minister leading the way to the hearse.

Music at a funeral home is often a problem, but since the usual funeral home has an organ, often the director can see that matters are taken care of.

Special Services

When a fraternal order is to have a part in a funeral, it should be clearly understood beforehand by all participants, including the minister. When a family asks a minister to conduct a funeral, the minister may properly assume charge of all the ceremonies connected with the event. The pastor will, of course, wish to be as considerate as possible of others who may also have been invited to take part. Misunderstanding and embarrassment may sometimes occur, unless there is a complete understanding before-hand regarding the part each is to assume. Common sense, not to say common sympathy, can usually be depended on to work out such matters. The tactful minister will have no trouble in making the lodge or veteran's organization feel that it has an essential part in the program, and they should in turn respect the pastoral position. Any such services may be held the evening before at the funeral home. In any case, the Christian ritual should come last.

Ministers are called upon from time to time to participate in formal *military funerals*. These may be extremely elaborate, and those who have served as chaplains in the armed forces can testify to what a rigid part protocol plays in such events. For instance, in the death of a local person whose friends wish to give him a military funeral, all details affecting the part the minister is to play in the service may easily be ascertained beforehand. Where an elaborate state funeral of some high-ranking officer is to be held, the military or naval marshal in charge may be depended on to give the minister—whether in uniform as a chaplain or out of it as pastor—directions and cues in each instance. The dramatic salute of the firing squad, if one is present, and the final sounding of taps by the bugler come after the chaplain (or minister) has pronounced the final benediction.

Memorial services are being used more and more today. The chief difference between a memorial service and a regular funeral service is that the body of the deceased is never present at a memorial service, and this forces a somewhat different pattern of procedure. None of the mechanics or movement of the usual funeral is in evidence, and those conducting the memorial rites must center their service and remarks definitely on the person memorialized. It is a service of worship. Generalities will not do here—the whole occasion is for the purpose of remembering and celebrating the life of a certain individual person.

Relationships with Funeral Directors

The minister and the funeral director share a joint responsibility in the management of a funeral. Theoretically, the minister has full charge of the rites and ceremonies in their spiritual significance and import, and as the conductor of an act of public worship also has a certain additional authority. The funeral director has charge of practical details and the mechanics of all events connected with the entire funeral occasion. Both persons are public functionaries and both, of course, must work together. While there have sometimes been complaints by ministers about officious funeral directors who overdramatize their professional function at funerals, most ministers see the funeral director as one who is sincerely trying to serve people who are in trouble and is endeavoring to perform professional services in a helpful way. Full and helpful cooperation between the two persons is always expected and is almost universally achieved.

9

MARRIAGES

Marriage is a rite that from time immemorial has been esteemed a religious one. In ancient times, the priest or minister was the sole judge as to who might be married, for there was no state license as at present. The priest or clergyman proclaimed "the banns" in public for a specified period, so that if there was any objection on the part of anyone, it might be stated and evaluated beforehand. If no objection was brought, and if the proposed marriage was in accord with the laws of the church, the priest or minister would then marry the couple. In all cases, the priest was the judge as to the right of matrimony.

Now, however, the state has come in, and the minister is no longer under the necessity of acting as a court to ascertain and proclaim the right of marriage between persons. The state's license clears the minister of civil obligations, but not of his or her own spiritual responsibility in this matter. The large denominations have made regulations governing the conduct of their ministers, but it may be said that the only situation in which the matter becomes acute today is the remarriage of divorced persons.

Divorced Persons and Remarriage

A large section of the Protestant ministry has always held that the "innocent party" to a divorce granted on the grounds of adultery might properly be married a second time to another. Ecclesiastical regulations of certain Protestant denominations have so allowed, though there have always been those who maintain that, while divorce is permissible and even necessary in some instances, remarriage is not. At the present time, there is a definite liberalizing of remarriage-after-divorce regulations on the part of certain large Protestant denominations. Ministers now recognize that a marriage may be broken for other reasons besides adultery.

Dr. Newman Smyth, in his *Christian Ethics,* held that there were sins that were "the moral equivalent" of adultery in disrupting marriage—habitual drunkenness, for instance, which "may utterly destroy the spiritual unity of a home and threaten even the physical security of one of the persons bound by the vows of marriage." The United Methodist Church, which in former days allowed ministers to remarry "the innocent party to a divorce whose true cause was adultery," now simply acknowledges divorce as "regrettable but recognizes the right of divorced persons to remarry."

Supporting this general attitude, though not these special regulations, are ministers of many faiths who have increasingly come to feel that the right of remarriage on the part of any divorced person is something that may not be dealt with by a general regulation, but by careful and considerate attention to each case. No matter how they differ as to the rules followed, ministers everywhere feel a sense of solemn concern for the whole problem of divorce and remarriage.

When a minister is asked to remarry a divorced person, there are three possible procedures:

1. *The minister can refuse to remarry any divorced*

person whatever the circumstances. This is the rule followed by a comparatively small number of ministers. It is not practiced by the vast majority.

2. *The minister can follow scrupulously the special ecclesiastical law of this church touching this whole matter.* About one-third of the ministers reporting their practice toward remarriage after divorce state that this is their procedure. Where church law is specific and directly applicable, ministers who owe it allegiance should be guided by it. The law of their church is their warrant, or their excuse, as the case may be.

3. *A minister can examine each cause on its own merits and in the light of the best knowledge available, decide whether it is right or wrong to perform the marriage of a divorced person.* This is apparently the practice of the great majority of Protestant ministers and of over two-thirds of the ministerial authorities relied on by this book. Many of these, of course, belong to denominations that do not provide exact regulations in this matter. Perhaps they may belong to the less centralized denominations, which cannot press upon their ministers any special rule or discipline. Some have the right under their church law to determine whether "vicious conditions" have broken the previous marriage of the presumably "innocent" party who now seeks remarriage. Naturally, any minister who undertakes to pass on the ins and outs of a divorce case assumes a tremendous responsibility. Mistakes are possible whatever decision is made.

In this situation, the best course is to ascertain all the facts bearing on the first marriage and the conditions that broke that marriage. Was there a genuine first marriage? Has there been an annulment or a divorce? How long has the divorce been granted? What do the legal papers say regarding the cause of the divorce? Above all, what do the people involved say? A private personal interview that deals with actual facts and that makes clear the intent of each person involved, rather than legal processes or public hearsay, will give the minister good guidance. If the decision is made conscientiously not to remarry the involved person, the pastor should say so, courteously and gently, but frankly and definitely. If, on the other hand, the decision is to go ahead, let it be done, not grudgingly or half doubtfully—the time for doubt is over—but as graciously and helpfully as would be done for any other marriage. The pastor's faith in the couple and expressed belief in their future may go far toward launching them into a well-founded new life.

Protestant ministers are not always aware of the ecclesiastical distinction between annulment and divorce. An annulment is a legal or ecclesiastical pronouncement that no valid marriage has ever taken place between two persons and that the supposed marriage between them is null and void. The ancient church worked out a whole series of regulations bearing on this matter and outlined the impediments that nullify a marriage. Blood relationship between the contracting parties within "forbidden degrees" of consanguinity; failure to consummate a marriage physically; insanity, if it can be proved to have existed before marriage, which keeps the afflicted party from entering into a valid marriage contract (but if insanity occurs after marriage, neither annulment nor divorce is allowed, as this comes under the "for better, for worse" vow); the existence of a previous unbroken marriage—these are among the causes for which the state and the ancient churches allowed annulment. The Roman Catholic Church, so strict on divorce, allows remarriage after annulment, but remains the judge as to the validity of the annulment. As state law and ancient canon law differ in some respects regarding annulment, the Protestant minister, who may not feel bound by either, will wish to review all facts in every case. Nevertheless if it is determined that the state has acted rightly in granting an annulment, the pastor may remarry the party concerned. Sometimes it may be found that a person has been given a divorce rather than an annulment, as the former was simpler to obtain; divorces have frequently been obtained by collusion between the parties when real causes have been concealed beneath pretended ones. The minister must in all cases get the actual facts, and act in accordance with them.

Elopements

Couples unknown to the minister sometimes ask to be married. The minister should be careful before consenting to perform the service. A candid conference between the pastor and the couple, sometimes with the intended bride alone, will often make the situation clear. Many ministers state that they refuse to perform elopements under any circumstances, though others feel that if the parties are properly qualified as to age and intelligence, and seem to know their own minds, they may well be married.

Elopements today have decreased as the states have become stricter in regard to the issuance of marriage licenses. Most require a certain time to elapse before a license can be used. Also, there are, in some instances, regulations as to health and blood tests that must be fulfilled before a marriage license is granted. These moves have served to discourage couples from a hasty and unplanned wedding. Ministers should remember, however, that occasionally there are couples who want to "slip away and be married quietly" for perfectly proper reasons—often financial.

Ethical Responsibility

The state will not and cannot force a minister to perform a marriage ceremony. Its license is an authorization, not a mandate. When a minister marries a couple, therefore, it is not possible to escape responsibility for the act by saying that if he or she does not, another minister will. This is simply to recall the Master's "it must needs be that offences come" and to forget the latter half of that pronouncement.

No minister worthy of the name should ever give the impression that the marriage service is simply a formula for a fee. "Marrying parsons" have brought discredit to the whole Christian community and to marriage itself in some localities. Those ministers who take part in unusual marriages or who perform the wedding ceremony in some spectacular place or manner are guilty of degrading an awe-ful and a sacramental act.

Nearly all denominations and ministers believe in and practice premarital counseling. This is a special time for the pastor to become even better acquainted with the bride and groom to be. In such intimate settings, the minister has the opportunity—and obligation—to impress upon the couple their spiritual commitment to God as they begin their new life together. It is a time to discuss the sacredness of home and family; a time to talk about budgets, shared responsibilities, and commitments of time and energy to each other as they covenant together to become "one under God."

There are many good books available in the area of premarital counseling. Suffice it to say that all of the following is built on the assumption that the pastor has spent sufficient time with the couple beforehand and that the minister will follow up appropriately with the couple once they have established their new home.

Preparing for a Marriage

The minister will do well to remember the role of being master of ceremonies at every wedding. Until the pronouncement of the final blessing, all must wait for the pastor's leadership. "Marriage consultants"—a highly specialized profession found in every city and often employed by large churches—family advisers, or such, may play a helpful part in the mechanics of a wedding, but the pastor must be in control of the actual service itself. The time is traditionally one of gaity, but anything like lightness or levity on the part of the minister, especially before the service, will detract much from the profession. A gracious dignity is the key to the pastor's whole demeanor.

The minister is expected to be an authority on everything connected with a wedding and is often referred to for advice on minor points having to do with the occasion. Thus it is advisable to obtain several authoritative books dealing with the proper procedure at a formal wedding. Many fine books are also available for the bride and groom to use in the planning (for instance, *Abingdon Marriage Manual* , rev. 1987 and *Marrying Again for Second Weddings*). These are a welcome gift to be given during the first premarriage counseling session.

The couple customarily decide the time and hour for the wedding and then request the use of the church. This should be done as many months as possible before the date, as church calendars fill up early. The pastor of the bride is usually asked to officiate. This, however, is not a fixed rule, as it may be that either bride or groom has a close relative who is a member of the clergy or one who is so closely tied to one of the families that this person will be selected for the occasion rather than the immediate pastor. In such circumstances, the wise pastor will, of course, understand. It is courteous in such situations for the parties to invite the pastor to have a part in the service. The invitation to the guest pastor should be extended through the bride's pastor.

If the wedding is to be held in a church and is to be somewhat formal, there is always a rehearsal. The minister, as well as the musicians, is expected to be present for this. The pastor will not only get to know the entire group in a much more intimate way during the rehearsal, but also will be able to induce a sense of security and ease by the assured way in which the arrangements are directed.

The minister is looked to for the proper direction of the entire rehearsal and should at once assume charge. The rehearsal may well begin by having the party posed *en tableau* at the chancel just as they will be when the ceremony is to begin; then, having gotten their respective positions in mind, the parties may go to the back of the church, the minister to the station by a side door, and the marches can commence and be repeated until all is satisfactory.

A Church Wedding

The church has been for ages the place in which matrimony is solemnized. In England, we are told, marriages rarely take place elsewhere. Many formal weddings are solemnized within a church. The church of the bride is the proper place for the wedding, though she may plan to leave it afterward for that of her husband.

Where the church is small, as in a village or rural community, or where the minister has no assistant, it may be necessary to give orders to the custodian regarding opening and preparing the church for the wedding. This should, of course, be done in plenty of time and the custodian instructed to be on hand at least an hour or two in advance to take care of necessary arrangements. The ushers for a formal wedding should be on hand forty-five minutes to an hour beforehand, though their instructions come from the bride and groom.

An examination of the marriage license by the minister at the rehearsal or earlier ought always to precede final preparation, if for no other reason than to see that the form is properly made out. Where the parties are well known to the minister, this may not be as necessary as when the wedding is for strangers, but carefulness always pays.

It will be supposed that the ushers have managed their duties well and that the wedding party has arrived at the church, where the bridesmaids and bride see that all is ready. In the meanwhile, the minister, with the groom and best man, is in the pastor's study awaiting the opening chord of the organ. If there is no pastor's study or private room, the pastor and groom may stand by a side door or remain in concealment until the minute arrives for them to take their respective places.

At the proper moment, the doors are opened for the wedding party or the signal agreed upon is given, and the wedding march begins. The minister walks slowly to a place within the chancel, facing the audience. Most ministers take their station before any of the bridal party have reached the chancel. A few ministers, however, state that they take their place just after the ushers have reached the chancel. The minister makes no attempt to keep pace with the music as the ushers and bridesmaids do. The minister goes out first, followed by the groom and best man, in that order, who stand to the left, half turned, watching for the entrance of the bride. It should be emphasized that the whole group forms on the minister, and the position is thus a guide to that of the others. When the bride arrives on the arm of her father, the groom usually takes a step or so to meet her. She releases her father's arm and puts her hand in that of the groom, and both take their places before the minister, who then advances a step toward them "book in hand." The bride's father then steps back and stands behind and to the left of the bride; the bridesmaids and groomsmen "close in" slightly, and the ceremony begins.

Ministers usually have their own manuals, rituals, or prayer books, directing them in the proper conduct of the marriage rite; even ministers of those denominations that do not prescribe any fixed office gradually evolve for themselves a regular form they use at each recurrent service. The usual ceremony, however, is that based on the

Office for the Solemnization of Matrimony, as ordered by the Prayer Book of the Church of England. The Episcopal Church in America has retained this office with some changes in the interest of brevity and delicacy of expression, neither of which was very pronounced in the old Prayer Book. The same office, slightly abridged, was transmitted to the Methodist Episcopal Church in America by John Wesley in his famous "Sunday Service," or Methodist liturgy of 1784. Through the Church of Scotland, this Anglican office also reached various Reformed churches, such as the Presbyterian Church (U.S.A.). This ancient office thus became the rite for a large group of American church people and has been the base of nearly all revised or individually evolved services. Lloyd C. Douglas once commended this ancient rite as the only one. "You will find," he said, "that all these home-brewed rituals lack a great deal of the dignity, power, and charm of the service to which I have referred." Hence, in order to outline the marriage service in the following pages, we may trace the successive steps of this ancient and magnificent ceremony.

From time immemorial the position of the man and woman when they are standing before the minister has been the same; the man on the right of the woman and the woman on the left of the man. This means that the woman is on the right of the minister and the man to the left.

The address with which this office opens is a general one and should be spoken to the entire audience in a sure, yet gracious, way. It is usually considered best for the minister to have in hand the ritual, manual, or prayer book and to make occasional reference to it. The pastor will be very familiar with the service and able, if need be, to repeat it from memory, but the book itself seems to give official dignity and sanction to this act. The majority of ministers today, about 75 percent of those describing their custom in this regard, state that they always "hold the book." To do so does make manifest a general churchly sanction that otherwise is lacking.

In recent years, the challenge to the audience ("If there be any who can show just cause why they may not lawfully be joined together, let him now speak.") and the challenge to the parties ("Do you know of any impediment why you may not lawfully be joined together?") have both been omitted by some from the marriage office, the principle being that the couple would not be standing there if they had not already satisfied both the civil authorities and their own consciences that there was nothing to prevent their marriage. But those who defend the ancient use here say that a marriage is all the more valid if it can be certified afterward that neither the world (represented by the audience) nor the couple, solemnly and publicly questioned, knew of any objection regarding it.

Since no reply in either case is anticipated, the minister at once goes into the *espousals*. This is the familiar, "Will you have this woman to be your wedded wife . . . ?" The given names are used—"John, will you have this woman. . . ?" "Mary, will you have this man. . . ?"

In previous centuries, the espousal or espousals preceded the marriage, sometimes by years. They corresponded in medieval times to what we now term "engagements." The espousal is the mutual promise and expression of willingness on the part of each person to take the other and "keep only unto each other" so long as both shall live.

Next in the ancient office comes the ceremony known as "giving away the bride," or in more modern language, the *"presenting into marriage of the woman."* The father or nearest male relative usually performs this service, though his participation is chiefly concerned with escorting the bride to the groom. This ceremony is not to be regarded as an outgrowth of the old custom of coemption, or buying of the bride by the groom, though some have contended that this was its origin. The language of the churchly office makes it plain that the father does not give his daughter to the man but *to be married* to the man. He gives her to the Church, represented by the minister, who in turn marries her to the man. The old York Rite from which this ceremony was taken and incorporated into the English office makes this plain: *Deinde sacerdos,* "Who gyves me thys wyfe?" The "wife" was given to the priest, who married her to the man.

In keeping with this idea, the father—when the minister asks, "Who gives this woman to be married to this man?"—steps forward and symbolically places the hand of the bride in that of the minister, who at once places it in the hand of the groom. Some rituals today, for example the United Methodist, provide an office in which the father responds, "I do," or "Her mother and I do," when this question is asked. The Protestant Episcopal use, and that of the Church of England, has never called for an audible response on the part of the relative who gives the bride in marriage, the symbolic giving of her hand to the minister and to the groom fulfilling this requisite. Until this part of the service, the father has been standing a half step behind and to the side of the bride. Now, after putting her hand in that of the minister, the father steps back to take his place with the bride's mother, or other family, in the seat provided.

It is at this point that that the true marriage, technically speaking, begins. In keeping with this idea, the officiating minister—that is, the one who is actually to marry the couple—now takes the service, if someone else had it from the beginning. Where there is another minister to assist, such an assistant is often given the conduct of the office up to this point—that is, beginning with the marriage address and through the giving into marriage of the woman. The majority of ministers who report their custom in this regard state that they so divide the service. However, quite a few state that they frequently assign the wedding prayer (in the last part of the service) to an assisting minister. Some ministers report that this whole matter of dividing the marriage service is a matter of indifference to them. Thus they say that when more than one minister is to take part in a wedding, let the two divide the service in any way that seems mutually agreeable. But tradition, powerful even among the nonliturgical ministers, calls for the actual marriage—that is the pledging of the troth and the pledging with the ring—to be conducted by the minister in charge.

Ministers should understand the dramatic movement underlying the successive steps of the marriage rite. The audience has been called to witness by the address; the parties have been challenged for obstacle; the espousals have been heard; the father has given away the bride; now the actual marriage can begin. In keeping with this idea, it has long been the custom of the clergy of the Church of England and of the Protestant Episcopal Church to turn at this point and, followed by the couple, proceed from the nave of the church up the steps to the altar. There the couple again stand and the rest of the ritual takes place. Clergy are divided about allowing others than the actual wedding couple to approach the altar, though a slight majority of those reporting their practice state that they do allow the best man and maid of honor to accompany the wedding couple to the altar. The bride must dispose of her bridal bouquet in order to have her left hand free for the ring, and the maid of honor can aid her at this point. The maid of honor and the best man are responsible for the wedding rings until this place in the ceremony.

Many nonliturgical churches have no facilities for this approach to the altar, as the chancel rail has no gate or opening, nor is there an altar arranged as in the Anglican or Protestant Episcopal churches. Therefore, in nonliturgical churches, or those with a center pulpit, the entire ceremony takes place before the chancel rail.

The betrothal now takes place and consists of a symbolic taking of hands and the repetition by each party of a betrothal speech: "I John take you Mary . . . " The printed rubric or general practice of each church governs in this matter, but it is often convenient for the minister to join the hands and to place a hand lightly upon the clasped hands of the bridal pair while they are "plighting the troth." In outlining the respective speeches of the couple, here as well as in the "ring ceremony," the minister had best proceed by short phrases rather than long ones.

The wedding, or "ring ceremony," is an ancient part of the marriage rite. In medieval times, the ring was blessed by the priest after the groom had said, "With this ringe I the wed, and this gold and siluer I the geue, and With my body I the Worshipe, and With all my worldly cathel I the endowe." He then put the ring on the woman's thumb, saying, "In the Name of the Father." Then he put the ring on the *secundo digito* (second finger), saying, "and of the Son"; on the third finger, saying, "and of the Holy Ghost"; and then on the fourth finger, saying, "Amen." Because of the blessing of the ring, as done in medieval times, the Puritans objected bitterly to the ring ceremony and the old Presbyterian Directory appeared without it. So also John Wesley removed the ring ceremony from the marriage rite he transmitted to America, and not until comparatively recent times did Presbyterians or Methodists in America replace this ceremony in their rituals. The Protestant Episcopal Church, of course, always had it and in 1928 put in an optional prayer for the blessing of the ring. The Methodist Church, since 1940, has inserted a little speech to be made by the minister regarding the ring and an optional prayer blessing, not of the ring, but of the giving of it. Most nonliturgical ministers today have no scruples against the "ring ceremony" even where their own service books do not include it. It is, in reality, a beautiful and symbolic act.

Those who follow strictly the intent and direction of the ancient office and its rubric in the "giving and receiving of a ring" arrange it so that the ring itself makes a circle among the parties involved. The ancient rubric outlined these steps: *"The man shall give [1] unto the woman a ring. . . . . And the minister, taking [2] the ring [from the woman] shall give [3] it to the man to put [4] it upon the fourth finger of the woman's left hand. And the man holding it there and taught by the minister shall say. . . ."*

The ancient rubric has been modified within recent years so that there is no mention of the woman's receiving the ring until the man puts it on her finger. The minister takes the ring from the groom, blesses it, or affirms it, or perhaps with no words at all gives it to the man to put on the woman's finger. In this ceremony, the minister again outlines the words the man must say.

It is interesting to observe that the word *wedding,* which properly belongs only to this ceremony, has been generalized to mean in modern parlance the entire marriage rite. As was indicated above, for a long time the Presbyterians and Methodists solemnized many a "marriage" that was not a "wedding." Whenever the groom weds—that is, pledges—the bride with a ring, there is a wedding. A "wed" was something given as a pledge in Old English, and a wedding was, of course, a pledging.

In a double ring ceremony, the giving of the ring by the woman follows immediately her wedding by the man. The manner in which the man's ring is given may be exactly duplicated in the giving of the ring by the woman.

The wedding prayer follows. Quite often, as has been indicated, when there is more than one minister, this prayer is given to one who is assisting. However, as a rule it is better for the officiating minister to proceed to the end, as the wedding prayer is very short and the pronouncement that a marriage has taken place and the final blessing really belong to the one who is chiefly responsible for the rite.

After the wedding prayer, there is a symbolic joining of hands again for the pronouncement of marriage. Many ministers at this point prefer to clasp together the joined hands of the couple while saying, "Those whom God has joined together, let no one put asunder," and then proclaim to all the fact of the marriage: "Forasmuch as John and Mary have consented. . . ."

The couple usually kneel for a final blessing or benediction by the minister, which may be given with uplifted hand. When they arise, the minister may congratulate the newly married pair, provided this is done in such a gracious way that the solemnity of the service just concluded will not be impaired. Then the organist begins the march, and the party goes out in reverse order from that in which it entered.

Inquiry as to how long a minister should remain "in position" after a formal wedding is over brought a great variety of answers from ministerial authorities. A few leave at once; a larger number go when the wedding party is well down the aisle; while a still larger number say they wait until the family has begun to withdraw. In all cases, the minister goes out unobtrusively and, of course, never goes down the aisle as a part of the wedding recessional. Sometimes the bride and groom and their wedding party remain in the foyer of the church for a few moments of informal reception as their friends leave. This is a custom that has much to commend it for those who do not find it possible to invite all their friends to a postwedding reception.

Double Wedding

A double wedding, sometimes planned when sisters are the brides, is unusually difficult for the minister. There are portions of the service that may be adapted and used for both couples, but there are also portions that specifically must be individualized—not to speak of four given names to remember, and these four to be properly matched at the crucial moments. Also the rings—certainly two, perhaps four!

Tradition calls for the elder sister and her groom to stand to the left of the minister, the younger sister and her groom on the right. The minister marries the older first.

The address, with a slight adaptation, may be read for both couples—"met to join together this man and this woman [nodding to the left couple] and this man and this woman [nodding to the right] in the holy estate of matrimony." Separate challenges must be given for each couple, and the espousals require a definite question to each of the four persons; likewise, there must be a separate giving in marriage for each pair. The betrothals, of course, are managed separately, and so are the weddings. The wedding prayer, with an adaptation to the two couples, can be read for both, but the pronouncement of marriage must be entirely separate for each couple. The benediction or blessing can be adapted for both.

Home Wedding

A home wedding may be made almost as formal as one in a church, if so desired. An area is arranged with flowers or candles at the end of the room reserved for the ceremony. The minister usually prefers to remain somewhat in seclusion until time for the marriage. Generally a room is assigned to the pastor. There should be enough time before the ceremony to arrange last-minute details with the couple.

At the appointed moment, the minister arrives at the designated place. The couple, with attendants and others, come in with a formal march, or in a less formal way if they have so decided. The details of the service as outlined in the church wedding may act as a guide here. Quite often it is arranged to have a reception for the bride and groom immediately after the ceremony; when this is the case, the minister, after congratulating the couple, moves from the scene unobtrusively. They turn to face the company and receive the congratulations of their friends and relatives.

Minor details, such as filling out the marriage license, and such, may be attended to in a careful way after the ceremony. A much less formal atmosphere pervades a wedding reception in the home, and the minister usually feels free to enter into the spirit of the occasion as any guest might.

Marriage at the Minister's Home

A few marriages still take place at the minister's home. In such cases, not only is the pastor the officiating person, but is also the host. The pastor's spouse may act as witness when the law requires a witness.

The minister's duty in dealing with elopements has already been discussed. Let it be supposed, however, that the pastor feels free to marry the couple who are now in the parsonage, manse, or rectory living room. The couple will stand together with their friends and attendants, if there are any, behind them. The ceremony is conducted while all stand, as there are no facilities for kneeling, even if one's particular service calls for the couple to kneel. The blessing may be given with uplifted hand and then the couple allowed to depart after the necessary papers have been filled out.

And may the lovely blessing with which each couple is endowed as they are allowed to depart be put here for all who use this book: May God the Father, God the Son, and God the Holy Ghost bless, preserve, and keep you. May the Lord, with his favor, graciously look upon you and so fill you with all spiritual benediction and grace, that you may so live in this life that in the world to come you may have life everlasting.

INDEX